Alan C. Lloyd
Director, Typing Instructional Services
Gregg Division
McGraw-Hill Book Company

Russell J. Hosler
Emeritus Professor
University of Wisconsin, Madison

Mary Margaret Hosler
Professor, College of Business and Economics
University of Wisconsin, Whitewater

Rebecca Ann Hall
Chairperson, Business and Office Education
Centerville High School
Centerville, Ohio

Gregg Division
McGraw-Hill Book Company

New York St. Louis Dallas San Francisco
Auckland Bogotá Düsseldorf Johannesburg
London Madrid Mexico Montreal New Delhi
Panama Paris São Paulo Singapore Sydney
Tokyo Toronto

personal typing
FOURTH EDITION

Sponsoring Editor:
Ella Pezzuti
Senior Editing Manager:
Elizabeth Huffman
Editors:
Fredric Dannen and Susan Norton
Art Director:
Frank Medina
Design Supervisor:
Karen Mino
Production Supervisor:
Laurence Charnow

Library of Congress Cataloging in Publication Data

Main entry under title:

Personal typing.

   Third ed. by A. C. Lloyd and R. J. Hosler.
   SUMMARY: A text providing a complete one-semester course in typewriting for students who plan to use their typing skill for personal rather than vocational use.
   1. Typewriting. [1. Typewriting] I. Lloyd, Alan C.
Z49.L73 1979   652.3'02   78-16865
ISBN 0-07-038208-5

contents

index

preface

HOW CAN YOU USE YOUR TYPING SKILL?

You will find that typing skill is one of the most useful skills you can have. It will make many writing or copying tasks easier to accomplish than would otherwise be possible. It is a skill that will stay with you throughout your life.

Personal Use. For classroom use or for use outside the classroom, you will find that typing your own reports and letters will save both time and money. Because you will be able to compose at the typewriter, you will find that your writing goes much faster too.

Career Use. You will find typing a salable skill for a part-time job while you are attending high school or college or at any other time in your life. If you work as a newspaper reporter, a librarian, or the manager of your own business, typewriting skill is invaluable.

Extra Benefits. Without even knowing it, you will be improving your spelling, punctuation, and writing skills as you learn to type.

HOW WILL YOU LEARN TO TYPE?

Typing skill is developed through a specific sequence of activities grouped in two phases.

Phase One. The mastery of the typewriter itself comes first. This involves learning to use the keyboard by touch, using the operating parts efficiently, and knowing the basic arrangements for typed copy on a page.

Phase Two. Once the machine operations are mastered, you will build speed and accuracy through a series of special drills. You will also learn how to vary basic arrangements to fit a particular communication you are typing, and you will learn an easy way to compose communications at the typewriter.

ORGANIZATION OF THIS TEXT

The topics in *Personal Typing* are organized in logical order, beginning with basic machine operations and ending with fairly complex research reports.

Parts. Personal Typing is divided into three main parts. The function and goals for each part are explained on part-opening pages. In brief, Part 1 covers basic machine operations and all keyboard characters; Part 2 presents various types of cards, tables, and letters; and Part 3 teaches how to set up short and long research reports. At the end of each part is a progress test to help you judge your progress.

Units. Within each part, the main topics are subdivided and treated in units. Each part contains four units. Each of the four units in Part 1 ends with a clinic, which reviews the keys learned up to that point.

Lessons. Units are divided into lessons designed to fit the class period. Each lesson begins with a short warmup drill to limber up and relax your fingers. The lesson then proceeds with new keys and skill-development drills, other new subject matter, and timed writings.

Lessons are planned so that the work falls into two fairly even time periods, approximately 20 minutes each. Thus it is easy to adapt lessons to the time available.

SPECIAL FEATURES

The following aids are built into this edition to help you become a competent typist.

Performance Goals. Each lesson clearly states the goals you should achieve in the lesson. The Skill Check with each lesson is written so that it may be used as a speed and accuracy goal checkpoint.

Controlled Copy. Skill-building drills and timed writings are controlled for length, difficulty, and alphabet coverage.

Special Drills. Special drills are included to improve finger motions to get speed and accuracy as high as possible. Drills provide intensive practice in down reaches, up reaches, adjacent letters, and one-hand motions, for example.

Large Print. The copy for typing in Part 1 appears in a large type size to help you adjust to the process of reading while typing.

Instant Scoring. Skill Checks include superior figures at counted intervals to make it easy to determine your typing speed.

Typing Tips. Typing tips for such activities as arranging copy and making corrections—as well as tips for using correct punctuation and English—are given with most lessons.

Visual Keys. Whenever you are learning a new arrangement (such as a letter setup), a miniature of the completed assignment is shown so that you can check the arrangement of the material.

Integrated Projects. Because learning is more meaningful when various segments fit together and make sense as a whole, two integrated projects are provided. The first one, at the end of Part 2, has two themes: a visiting day at a college campus and a survey of typing classes. The second one, at the end of Part 3, is a research report on occupations.

Handwritten and Typed Draft Copy. Because much of the material copied for personal-use typing consists of handwritten or typed drafts, this edition includes a number of assignments to give practice in typing from drafts.

ACKNOWLEDGMENTS

The authors are grateful to the students and teachers who used the Third Edition and contributed suggestions for this new edition.

Alan C. Lloyd
Russell J. Hosler
Mary Margaret Hosler
Rebecca Ann Hall

TIMED WRITING GRADING SCALE

To learn in what aspects of typing you are strongest and weakest, you may use this grading plan. An "A" grade is *excellent;* "B" is *very good;* "C" is *good,* or *normal;* and "D" is *fair.*

Follow these steps to evaluate your timed writings:

1. To determine how many points you have earned for your accuracy:
a. Figure the total words you typed; then find the corresponding *line* in Table 1.
b. Count the total number of errors you made; then find the corresponding *column* in Table 1.
c. Note the number where the line and the column intersect; this number is your *percent of error* score. Example: 138 words with 4 errors would give a 3.0 *percent of error* score.

Table 1. Percent of Error

Total Words Typed	Number of Errors									
	1	2	3	4	5	6	7	8	9	10
50– 60	1.8	3.6	5.5	7.2	9.1	10.9	12.7	14.5	16.4	18.2
61– 70	1.5	3.1	4.6	6.2	7.7	9.2	10.8	12.3	13.8	15.4
71– 80	1.3	2.7	4.0	5.3	6.7	8.0	9.3	10.7	12.0	13.3
81– 90	1.2	2.4	3.5	4.7	5.9	7.1	8.2	9.4	10.6	11.8
91–100	1.1	2.1	3.2	4.2	5.3	6.3	7.4	8.4	9.5	10.5
101–110	1.0	1.9	2.9	3.8	4.8	5.7	6.7	7.6	8.6	9.5
111–120	.9	1.7	2.6	3.5	4.3	5.2	6.1	7.0	7.8	8.7
121–130	.8	1.6	2.4	3.2	4.0	4.8	5.6	6.4	7.2	8.0
131–140	.7	1.5	2.2	3.0	3.7	4.4	5.2	5.9	6.7	7.4
141–150	.7	1.4	2.1	2.8	3.4	4.1	4.8	5.5	6.2	6.9
151–160	.6	1.3	1.9	2.6	3.2	3.9	4.5	5.2	5.8	6.5
161–170	.6	1.2	1.8	2.4	3.0	3.6	4.2	4.8	5.5	6.0
171–180	.6	1.1	1.7	2.3	2.9	3.4	4.0	4.6	5.1	5.7
181–190	.5	1.1	1.6	2.2	2.7	3.2	3.8	4.3	4.9	5.4
191–200	.5	1.0	1.5	2.1	2.6	3.1	3.6	4.1	4.6	5.1
201–210	.5	1.0	1.5	2.0	2.4	2.9	3.4	3.9	4.4	4.9
211–220	.5	.9	1.4	1.9	2.3	2.8	3.3	3.7	4.2	4.7
221–230	.4	.9	1.3	1.8	2.2	2.7	3.1	3.6	4.0	4.4
231–240	.4	.9	1.3	1.7	2.1	2.6	3.0	3.4	3.8	4.3
241–250	.4	.8	1.2	1.6	2.0	2.4	2.9	3.3	3.7	4.1
251–260	.4	.8	1.2	1.6	2.0	2.4	2.7	3.1	3.5	3.9
261–270	.4	.8	1.1	1.5	1.9	2.3	2.6	3.0	3.4	3.8
271–280	.4	.7	1.1	1.5	1.8	2.2	2.5	2.9	3.3	3.6
281–290	.4	.7	1.1	1.4	1.8	2.1	2.5	2.8	3.2	3.5
291–300	.3	.7	1.0	1.4	1.7	2.0	2.4	2.7	3.1	3.4

d. Now, using the appropriate part of Table 2, see how many accuracy points you have earned. A 3.0 score would give 9 points in Lessons 1–25, 8 in Lessons 26–50, 6 in Lessons 51–75.

Table 2. Accuracy Points

Lessons 1–25 (2 Minutes)		Lessons 26–50 (3 Minutes)		Lessons 51–75 (5 Minutes)	
% Error	Points	% Error	Points	% Error	Points
0.0–2.5	10	0.0–2.0	10	0.0–1.0	10
2.6–3.1	9	2.1–2.6	9	1.1–1.5	9
3.2–3.8	8	2.7–3.3	8	1.6–2.0	8
3.9–4.5	7	3.4–4.0	7	2.1–2.5	7
4.6–5.5	6	4.1–5.0	6	2.6–3.3	6
5.6–6.5	5	5.1–6.0	5	3.4–4.1	5
6.6–7.5	4	6.1–7.0	4	4.2–5.0	4
7.6–8.5	3	7.1–8.0	3	5.1–6.0	3
8.6–9.5	2	8.1–9.0	2	6.1–7.0	2
9.6–9.9	1	9.1–9.9	1	7.1–8.0	1

2. Using the appropriate part of Table 3, see how many speed points you have earned. Example: 29 words a minute in Lessons 1–25 would earn 6 points; in Lessons 26–50, 5 points; and in Lessons 51–75, 3 points.

Table 3. Speed Points

Lessons 1–25 (2 Minutes)		Lessons 26–50 (3 Minutes)		Lessons 51–75 (5 Minutes)	
Speed	Points	Speed	Points	Speed	Points
35 up	10	40	10	45	10
33–34	9	38–39	9	43–44	9
31–32	8	36–37	8	41–42	8
30	7	35	7	40	7
28–29	6	31–34	6	37–39	6
26–27	5	28–30	5	34–36	5
23–25	4	25–27	4	30–33	4
20–22	3	23–24	3	28–29	3
17–19	2	20–22	2	25–27	2
15–16	1	18–19	1	23–24	1

3. Add your accuracy points and your speed points and grade the total on this scale:

Total Points:	2-6	7-12	13-17	18 or more
Grade Earned:	D	C	B	A

PART ONE

As you learn to typewrite, you will learn to control the machine and all its unique parts. Through systematic practice, you will become a competent typist who can use the typewriter as a valuable tool for writing personal notes, letters, and reports. You might even find that your skill will help you when you apply for a job.

Part One consists of four units. Unit 1 (Lessons 1–6) and Unit 2 (Lessons 7–12) introduce you to the keyboard and cover the alphabet. Unit 3 (Lessons 13–18) presents the number keys and provides instruction for and exercises in horizontal and vertical centering of lines and paragraphs. In Unit 4 (Lessons 19–24), you will learn the symbol keys, how to construct special symbols, and how to apply certain English style rules for symbols, such as where to place punctuation in relation to quotation marks and how to divide words correctly when you need to hyphenate.

A *clinic* comes at the end of each unit. The use of the clinics is explained before Clinic A at the end of Unit 1.

Each part is followed by a progress test, which provides exercises that will help you to determine your competency in the skills emphasized in the part.

When you have completed Part One, you will be able to:
1. Use correct stroking patterns and maintain good posture to control keys by touch.
2. Operate the margin controls, spacing controls, scales, locks and releases, backspace key, tabulator, and other production mechanisms that are part of the machine.
3. Arrange a message on a page using vertical and horizontal centering, indenting, all capitals, aligning, and underscoring.
4. Type 25 words a minute for 2 minutes with 4 or fewer errors.

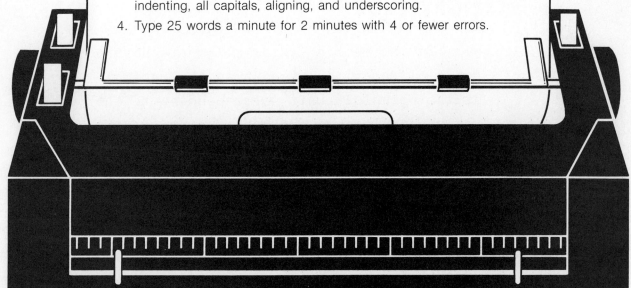

PENALTY SCALE

−3 problem is off center vertically or horizontally
−3 line-spacing instruction was not followed
−3 words or lines were omitted
−2 paragraph or display line is not indented properly
−2 display line is not centered
−1 strikeover, incorrect letter or symbol, space omitted, raised capital, or similar typing error

The Metric System[1]

Prepared for History I
A Report by Cathy Elliott

INTRODUCTION

People through out the world measure lengths, distances, weights, and other values by a standard method called the metric system. A group of french scientists developed the metric system. France adopted it as the legal system of weights and measures in 1979. It was not until 1837 that its use was made compulsory. After World War II, many other countries adopted the metric system including China, Egypt, and India. In the 1960's, Great Britain and most of the Commonwealth of Nations began to convert to the system. The United States is among the last of the major countries of the world to convert to the metric system.

HOW THE METRIC SYSTEM IS ORGANIZED[2]

In the metric system all units have a uniform scale of relation, based upon the decimal. The meter is the principal unit which corresponds to the yard as a unit of measure. The scale of multiples and subdivisions of the meter is ten. All units of measurement are derived from the meter.

s.s. 1. The World Book Encyclopedia, Field Enterprises Educational Corporation, Chicago, 1968, p. 360.

s.s. 2. Charles Witson, "Let's Go To Metric," Nowadays Guide, April, 1977, pp. 34–39.

introducing the typewriter

goals

Learn the names, location, and function of the main parts of your typewriter. ☐ Learn procedure for centering, inserting, and removing paper. ☐ Set margins. ☐ Set spacing regulator.

Carriage. Top moving section that holds paper.

Carriage Release. Lever that allows carriage to move freely from side to side.

Carriage or Carrier Return Key (electric) or Carriage Return Lever (manual). Used for returning carriage or carrier.

Carriage Scale or Carrier Scale. Gauge that counts and numbers spaces.

Carrier Position Indicator. Small triangle that points to position of carrier on scale.

Cylinder. Large roller that holds paper.

Cylinder Knob. Wheel used to turn cylinder by hand.

Element. Sphere with alphabet and symbols.

Margin Scale. Scale used to determine where to set margins.

Margin Set. Key, button, or lever used to set margin stops.

Paper Bail. Rod that holds rollers that keep paper in place.

Paper Guide. Blade against which left edge of paper rests.

Paper Guide Scale. Scale that shows position of paper guide.

Paper Release. Lever used to remove or straighten paper.

Print Point. Point where typebar or element strikes paper.

Spacing Regulator. Lever that controls space between lines of type.

Variable Spacer. Button in left cylinder knob used to raise or lower paper.

MAIN TYPEWRITER PARTS

▷ **Locate the parts labeled in the drawings and learn the function of each part.**

TYPEBAR MACHINE

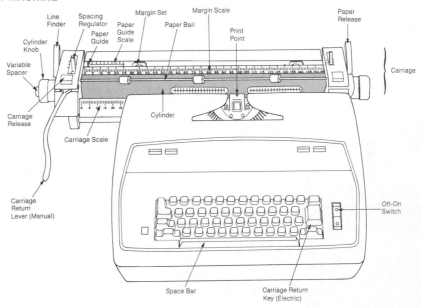

ELEMENT MACHINE

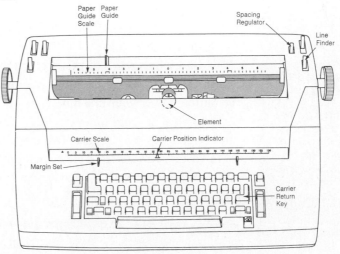

2

part three progress test

goals

Type memorandum with enumerations. □ Type manuscript with reference notes. □ Type 35 wam for 5 minutes within 4 errors.

TYPING TIPS
□ A heading block for a memorandum has these guide words: *To, Subject, From, Date.*
□ A footnote may be placed at the point where it applies in the report, at the foot of the page, or at the end of the report.

SKILL CHECK

▶ Can you type 35 words a minute in a 5-minute timing with 4 or fewer errors?

1	The sport of racing can take on many meanings and many	12
2	forms for different people. One may talk about horse races	24
3	or dog races, turtle races or rabbit races, or maybe even a	36
4	zebra or a quail will race. Whatever animal you might name	48
5	may be capable of one kind of race or another. People race	60
6	on foot, on skis, on bicycles, and on skates. They race in	72
7	autos, in airplanes, and in sailboats. The chance to win a	84
8	lot of money may be the reason that some people like races,	96
9	but for others it is just the excitement of seeing a fierce	108
10	contest and cheering the favorite on to victory. And still	120
11	others like to look at the sleek racehorses or the colorful	132
12	sails, or they come just to lend support to a friend who is	144
13	in the contest.	147
14	In some races the talent of the handler, or driver, is	159
15	what counts. That talent will win the admiration of people	171
16	who attend the race.	175

|1 |2 |3 |4 |5 |6 |7 |8 |9 |10 |11 |12 **SI: 1.39**

PROBLEM 1. MEMORANDUM WITH ENUMERATIONS

▶ Type in correct form, supplying the appropriate headings and to-day's date. Write the memo to a classmate from you.

5-inch line.

Everyone who uses a typewriter should know how to keep it in good operating condition. Cover your machine at night to help protect it and prevent dust from gathering on and in it. Just like any piece of furniture, it needs to be cleaned. Use the following guide to keep it in good operating condition:

1. Once each day the element or typebars should be cleaned with a stiff brush or commercial product made for this purpose.

2. Each week use a soft cloth moistened with oil to wipe off the metal rails on which the carriage or the carrier moves.

3. About every two weeks use a cloth dampened with alcohol to clean the cylinder.

If you follow these tips, your machine will give you good service.

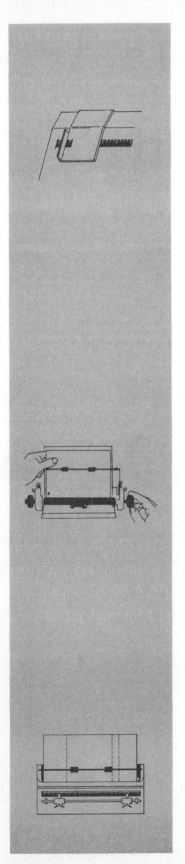

SETTING THE PAPER GUIDE

You must learn to set the paper guide so that a sheet of paper, when inserted, will center at 50 on the scales.

Take these eight steps to position the guide properly. (You need to do this only once since you will know where the paper guide belongs after this.)

1. Move the paper guide as far to the left as it can go.
2. Set the carriage or carrier at 50.
3. Pull the paper bail forward or up.
4. Crease the center of the paper at the top.
5. Holding the sheet in your left hand, set it behind the cylinder, and draw it into the machine by turning the knob with your right hand.
6. After depressing the paper release to loosen the paper, slide the paper left or right until the center crease is at the printing point.
7. Slide the paper guide to the right until its upright blade edge is against the side of the sheet of paper.
8. Note on the guide scale exactly where you have set the paper guide. If you always keep the paper guide at this position, you will be sure that any time you insert a sheet of paper in your typewriter, it will center at 50.

INSERTING AND REMOVING PAPER

The routine for inserting and removing your paper has seven steps.

1. Check to see that the paper guide is in the correct position.
2. Pull the paper bail forward or up.
3. With your left hand, put the paper behind the cylinder and against the paper guide; now use your right hand to turn the right cylinder knob to draw in the paper. Move the paper forward until about a third of it can be seen.
4. Check to see if the paper is straight by pressing the top part of your paper against the bottom part; the top and bottom should line up at the paper guide. If they do not, loosen the paper (use the paper release) and straighten it.
5. Put the paper bail back against the paper. Adjust the rollers on the bail so that they divide the paper in thirds.
6. Turning the right-hand cylinder knob, roll the paper until only a quarter inch or so shows above the bail. Now the paper is in position for typing the warmups at the beginning of each session.
7. When you remove the paper, pull the bail forward or up. Then depress the paper release (right hand) as you pull out the sheet of paper (left hand).

SETTING MARGINS

Margin stops at the sides of a typed page control the margins by limiting the line of writing. The length of the writing line you are to use will always be indicated. "40-space line," for example, means that you are to set the margin stops for a line of 40 spaces. Plan the left and right margin settings separately.

Left Margin. Subtract half the desired line from the center. For a 40-space line, 50 (center) − 20 (half of 40) = 30, the scale point at which the left margin stop is to be set.

Right Margin. Add half the desired line and 5 extra spaces (an allowance for line-ending adjustments) to the center. For a 40-space line, for example, 50 (center) + 20 (half of 40) + 5 = 75, the point at which the right margin stop is to be set.

3

COMPLETING THE RESEARCH PAPER

Type a title page or cover page, a table of contents, a list of tables, and a bibliography.

1. Use your judgment in the arrangement of the information on the title page. (Refer to page 106 for examples.)
2. Use leaders in the table of contents.
3. Use leaders in the list of tables.
4. Compose the bibliography from the 3″ x 5″ cards illustrated below.
5. Organize the pages of the paper and staple them together at the left or punch holes at the left and place them in a notebook binder.

Turn in the original to your teacher and keep the carbon copy. You now have a complete paper with all parts available for you to use as a model for future papers you may have to prepare.

Occupational Outlook Handbook, 1976-77,
Department of Labor
Verified job categories, but did not quote. Use this in bibliography.

Archer, Fred C., et al., *General Office Procedures*, 4th ed., McGraw-Hill Book Company, New York, 1975.

quote from page v.
Placed in report just before Table 3 (first two sentences). Include as footnote and in bibliography.

"Jobs With the Brightest Future," *Changing Times*, September, 1977, pp. 6-11.

All information for tables comes from this article. Direct quote is the second paragraph in the Summary. Include as footnote to each table and in bibliography.

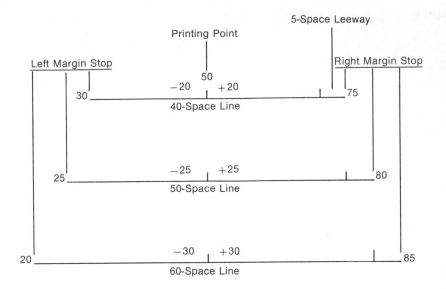

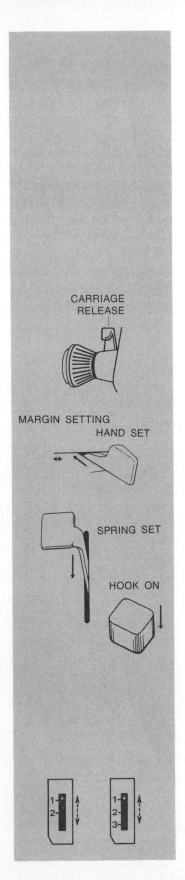

CARRIAGE
RELEASE

MARGIN SETTING
HAND SET

SPRING SET

HOOK ON

To move the carriage freely left or right, (1) brace your left hand against the left cylinder knob as you (2) press the adjacent carriage release lever. You can use this method when you move the carriage to set left and right margins. The chart above shows where to set margins for a 40-, 50-, or 60-space line.

Spring-Set Margin Stops. Royals, Smith-Coronas, and some Allens have a margin set lever at each end of the carriage. For the left margin, (1) pull forward and hold the left margin set lever, (2) move the carriage to the desired scale position, and (3) release the set key. For the right margin, (1) pull forward and hold the right margin set lever, (2) move the carriage to the desired scale point, and (3) release the set key.

Hand-Set Margin Stops. Margin stops of Underwoods, IBM Selectrics, Olympias, Remingtons, some Allens, and most portables are adjusted by hand without use of a set key. Set each margin stop separately: (1) press down or in on the margin stop, (2) slide the stop right or left to the desired scale point, and (3) release the margin stop.

Hook-On Margin Stops. Electric Underwoods, typebar IBMs, and some Remingtons have hook-on margin stops. For the left margin, (1) move the carriage to the left margin, (2) hook onto the left margin stop by holding down the margin set key on the keyboard, (3) move the carriage to the desired scale point, and (4) release the set key. For the right margin, (1) move the carriage to the right margin, (2) hook onto the right margin stop by holding down the set key on the keyboard, (3) move the carriage to the desired point, and (4) release the set key.

▷ **Set your margins for a 40-space line, using the procedure for your typewriter.**

SETTING THE SPACING REGULATOR

The blank space between the lines of typing is controlled by the spacing regulator. Set it at 1 for single spacing, which provides no blank space between typed lines, and at 2 for double spacing, which provides 1 blank line between typed lines. Many machines also provide for $1\frac{1}{2}$ spacing, $2\frac{1}{2}$ spacing, and/or 3 spacing. Most typing is single- or double-spaced.

Set at 1	Set at 2
Single	Double
Single	
Single	Double
Single	

▷ **Set your spacing regulator for single spacing.**

4

E. Service

Many service occupations # continue to grow as the population increases.

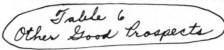
Table 5
Service Occupations

F. OTHER GOOD PROSPECTS

A number of other jobs report growth and are worth looking into. These are tabulated below.

Table 6
Other Good Prospects

G. LESS ENCOURAGING PROSPECTS

There are some occupations which report no change or an actual decline in the number of annual openings. Although competition will be strong in the following areas, not much growth is expected: # electrotypers, stereotypers, and photoengravers; boiler tenders and stationary engineers; postal clerks and mail # carriers; college and university professors; kindergarten, elementary, and secondary teachers; college career placᵉment counselors and interpreters.

IV. Summary

The less education and training a person has, the less chance he *or she* has for a job with a *good* future. On the other hand, the projected supply of college graduates through the mid-1980's will exceed the *anticipated* demand for them.

College graduates are more likely to experience underemployment (jobs that do not fully utilize their talents and training) and job dissatisfaction. Some analysts think that will be a *greater* problem for the grads than outright unemployment because the degree will always provide an edge in competition for jobs. ②

Therefore, it is more important that students match their course work with the job # market than it has ever been in the past.

This paragraph is a direct quote. Consider the length before deciding how to set it up. Information for the footnote is on p. 136.

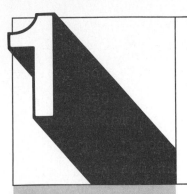

goals

Sit in correct typing position with hands in correct "home position."
□ Control home keys and space bar without looking at them.

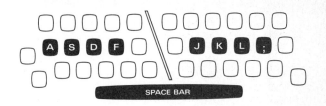

Are you sitting like the typist illustrated below?

CORRECT POSTURE

Head. Erect and facing the book, which should be at the right of the machine and tilted to reduce shine on paper.

Back. Straight with body leaning forward slightly; shoulders level.

Body. A handspan from the machine, centered opposite the J key.

Feet. Apart, firmly braced on the floor, one foot ahead of the other.

Fingers. Curved under so only tips touch the keys.

POSITION OF HANDS ON HOME KEYS

Left Hand. Place your fingertips on the **A S D** and **F** keys.

Right Hand. Place your fingertips on the **J K L** and **;** keys.

Curve the fingers so that only their tips touch the keys. Your fingers are named for the home keys on which they rest. For example, the fourth finger of your left hand is the A finger.

Thumbs. Strike the space bar with the thumb of your writing hand. Whichever thumb you use should be poised a half inch above the middle of the space bar. The other thumb is not used; hold it close to its adjacent forefinger.

USING THE SPACE BAR

With all fingers motionless on or slightly above the home keys, and with both hands as low as you can hold them without having your palms or wrists touch the front of the machine, sharply tap the space bar with your thumb. Make the thumb bounce off the space bar. Practice spacing according to the following instructions.

Space once (*tap the space bar once*) . . . twice (*tap the space bar twice*) . . . once . . . once . . . twice . . . once . . . twice . . . once . . . twice . . . twice . . . once . . . once . . . . **Repeat once more.**

Manual Return

Electric Return

USING THE CARRIAGE OR CARRIER RETURN

Manual Machine. Place the left forefinger and the next two fingers against the return lever. Move the lever with a flick of the wrist to return the carriage to the margin, and return the hand to home key position.

Electric Machine. Extend the Sem finger to the return key. Lightly press the key, causing the carriage or carrier to return automatically, and return the finger to home key position.

▶ **Practice returning the carriage or carrier.**

Space once . . . twice . . . once . . . twice. . . . Ready to return (*move hand to return lever or finger to return key*). Return! (*Return the carriage or carrier.*) . . . Home! (*Place fingers on home keys.*) . . . **Repeat.**

You will need Tables 5 and 6 for the portion of the report that is on text page 135.

Mechanics and Repair

Industrial Machinery Repairers - 42,500

Maintenance Electricians - 13,800

Air-conditioning, Refrigeration, & Heating Mechanics - 10,900

Instrument Repairers - 6,600

TV & Radio Service Technicians - 4,300

Computer Service Technicians - 4,300

Diesel Mechanics - 3,400

Business Machine Repairers - 3,100

Boat-Motor Mechanics - 550

Table 4

Service

Cooks and Chefs - 78,600

Police Officers - 22,000

Bartenders - 15,200

Health & Regulatory Inspectors - Govt. - 7,900

State Police Officers - 3,600

Construction Inspectors - Govt. - 1,700

Occupational Safety & Health Workers - 1,100

Table 5

Other Good Prospects

Manufacturing Inspectors - 51,000

Social Workers - 30,500

Operating Engineers - 27,000

Welders - 27,000

Plumbers and Pipe Fitters - 23,700

Construction Electricians - 11,700

Social Service Aides - 8,400

Wastewater Treatment Plant Operators - 6,100

Recreation Workers - 5,900

Architects - 3,000

Table 6

▶ Practice stroking forefinger keys and space bar.

Strike the F and J and space strokes shown in the drill lines below. Experiment to see how hard you must tap the keys to get them to print evenly. Type each line once.

Left forefinger, stroking thumb

fff fff ff ff f f ff ff f f **Return.**

Right forefinger, stroking thumb

jjj jjj jj jj j j jj jj j j **Return twice.**

LEFT HAND

Forefinger . . . . F
Second finger . . D
Third finger . . . . S
Fourth finger . . . A

Space Bar . . . Left thumb
if you are left-handed.

RIGHT HAND

J . . . . . Forefinger
K . . .Second finger
L . . . . Third finger
; . . . . Fourth finger

Space Bar . . . Right
thumb if you are right-
handed.

▶ **Set your machine for a 40-space line and single spacing. Type each line three times, as shown. Double-space between *different* lines.**

F AND **J** KEYS

Use forefingers and stroking thumb.

1 fff jjj fff jjj fj fj fff jjj ff jj f j
2 fff jjj fff jjj fj fj fff jjj ff jj f j
3 fff jjj fff jjj fj fj fff jjj ff jj f j

D AND **K** KEYS

Use second fingers.

4 ddd kkk ddd kkk dk dk ddd kkk dd kk d k
5 ddd kkk ddd kkk dk dk ddd kkk dd kk d k
6 ddd kkk ddd kkk dk dk ddd kkk dd kk d k

S AND **L** KEYS

Use third fingers.

7 sss lll sss lll sl sl sss lll ss ll s l
8 sss lll sss lll sl sl sss lll ss ll s l
9 sss lll sss lll sl sl sss lll ss ll s l

A AND **;** KEYS

Use fourth fingers.

10 aaa ;;; aaa ;;; a; a; aaa ;;; aa ;; a ;
11 aaa ;;; aaa ;;; a; a; aaa ;;; aa ;; a ;
12 aaa ;;; aaa ;;; a; a; aaa ;;; aa ;; a ;

NEW KEY REINFORCEMENT

Try to return the carriage or carrier without looking up.

13 aaa sss kkk ask ddd aaa ddd dad ask dad
14 aaa sss kkk ask ddd aaa ddd dad ask dad
15 aaa sss kkk ask ddd aaa ddd dad ask dad

These library reference cards contain the data for the tables you are to insert in the report.

Do not abbreviate words or use the ampersand for *and*.

Scientific and Technical

Degree

Electrical Engineers - 12,200
Civil Engineers - 9,300
Mechanical Engineers - 7,900
Industrial Engineers - 7,200
Chemical Engineers - 1,850
Physicists - 1,700
Geologists - 1,300
Statisticians - 1,250
Biochemists - 800
Petroleum Engineers - 750
Geophysicists - 450
Ceramic Engineers - 350
Food Scientists - 350
Biochemical Engineers - 150

Table 2

Nondegree   Table 2

Engineering & Science Technicians - 32,000
Drafters - 17,300
Surveyors - 3,600

Office

Secretaries & Stenographers - 439,000
Typists - 125,000
Bank Clerks - 54,000
Bank Tellers - 30,000
Personnel and Labor Relations Workers - 23,000
Computer Operators - 16,400
Bank Officers - 16,000
Computer Programmers - 13,000
Purchasing Agents - 11,700
Systems Analysts - 9,100
Buyers - 9,000
Collection Workers - 4,500
Credit Managers - 4,500
Marketing Research Workers - 3,000
Urban Planners - 100

Table 3

16 sss aaa ddd sad lll aaa ddd lad sad lad

17 sss aaa ddd sad lll aaa ddd lad sad lad

18 sss aaa ddd sad lll aaa ddd lad sad lad

19 fff aaa ddd fad aaa sss ;;; as; fad ask

20 fff aaa ddd fad aaa sss ;;; as; fad ask

21 fff aaa ddd fad aaa sss ;;; as; fad ask

goals

Control H, E, and O keys. □ Type 60 strokes or more in 1 minute.

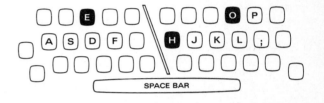

▷ **40-space line; single-space; each line three times; double-space between *different* lines.**

WARMUP

1 aaa ;;; sss lll ddd kkk fff jjj aaa ;;;

2 lad ask fad as; fad dads asks lads fads

H KEY

Use J finger.

3 jjj jhj hhh jjj jhj hhh jjj jhj hhh jhj

4 jhj has has jhj ash ash jhj had had jhj

5 has had ha; ha; had has ha; ha; ah; ah;

E KEY

Use D finger.

6 ddd ded eee ddd ded eee ddd ded eee ded

7 ded fed fed ded led led ded elf elf ded

8 elk elk he; he; ale ale sea sea eel eel

O KEY

Use L finger.

9 lll lol ooo lll lol ooo lll lol ooo lol

10 lol old old lol sod sod lol oak oak lol

11 doe doe ode ode foe foe hoe hoe so; so;

NEW KEY REINFORCEMENT

12 hhh she she she ha; ha; ha; has has has

13 eee hoe hoe hoe sea sea sea lee lee lee

14 ooo sod sod sod old old old ode ode ode

15 half half soak soak safe safe jade jade

▷ **Type the remaining pages that make up the research paper. Make corrections and insert tables as indicated.**

Tables 2 and 3 are on text page 133 and Table 4 is on page 134. You should study the tables and plan how to set them up *before* you begin to type.

Use *Ibid.* for the source for Table 2. Since a footnote comes between Tables 2 and 3, repeat the complete information on the source of the table below Table 3. (Copy it from Table 1.)

The writer indicated a footnote by the encircled number 1. You decide where to place footnotes (refer to pages 119–120 for help). Data for the footnote is shown on an index card on text page 136.

Other ^health^ occupations which are growing rapidly are: licensed practical nurses, occupational therapists, occupational therapy assistant ^s and^ , physical therapy assistants and aides.

B. TECHNICAL AND SCIENTIFIC

Many of the scientific jobs in engineering and science require a college degree or more. The jobs reported in this category will be divided by degree and nondegree jobs.

Table 2
Scientific and Technical Occupations

C. OFFICE

s.s. Offices in business, government, and industry offer an extraordinary number and variety of opportunities for immediate employment. The expansion of office staffs and the replacement of workers in various clerical positions results in an increasing demand for hundreds of thousands of new typists, general office clerks, file clerks, payroll clerks, messengers, and other vitally important employees each year. ①

Students who have intensive training in high school can expect to ^have^ good paying jobs immediately after high school. Many jobs [have that] been traditionally held by men are now opening up to women ⸰ also.

Table 3
Office Occupations

D. MECHANICS AND REPAIR

Most of the jobs in this category are in industry and require on-the-job training and/or up to four years of apprenticeship work.

Table 4
Mechanics and Repair Occupations

POSTURE CHECKLIST

Study the photograph in the margin. Ask one of your classmates to watch you as you type the next one or two drill lines. Check for each of the 10 points of good posture that are listed below. Then you do the same for your classmate.

1. Head erect; eyes on book.
2. Shoulders relaxed.
3. Upper arms and elbows hang loosely, close to sides of body.
4. Forearms on same slant as the keyboard.
5. Sitting well back on chair, leaning forward slightly from hips.
6. Both feet resting squarely on floor and spread apart.
7. Body centered opposite the J key.
8. Fingers curved over the keys.
9. Wrists about a half inch above the machine.
10. Sitting about a handspan from typewriter.

▶ **40-space line; single-space; each line three times or more; double-space between *different* lines.**

WORD PRACTICE

16 has has fed fed elk elk oak oak he; he;
17 hoe hoe ask ask old old she she ode ode
18 hod hod fee fee oh; oh; had had doe doe
19 so; so; lee lee ash ash elf elf sea sea

20 soda soda lake lake jell jell safe safe
21 sold sold fled fled seal seal joke joke
22 hole hole jade jade hold hold seal seal
23 fake fake lead lead soak soak fold fold

24 she shoe shad; fee fed fell; do doll; a
25 all alas; la lad lash; elk elf; he heed
26 held; of off; jade jake; sod sole sold;
27 dash dale; ash ashes ask; sad sale sake

▶ **There are 60 strokes altogether in lines 28 and 29. Try to type them within 1 minute. If you finish line 29 before the minute is over, start again on line 28. Try this timing at least three times.**

SKILL CHECK

28 feel sad; do ask a fee; dad has a joke;
29 flee foes; see jade;

A. HEALTH

The fastest-growing occupation in the health services area is the dental assistant. There are excellent opportunities for graduates of one- and two-year programs for both full-time and part-time employment.

A number of other health service occupations offer good prospects for the future.

Table 1

HEALTH OCCUPATIONS*
↓1

Occupation	Number of Jobs Expected
↓2	↓1 ↓2
Licensed Practical Nurses	93,000
Registered Nurses	71,000
Medical Assistants	27,200
Physicians and Osteopathic Physicians	23,000
Medical Lab Workers	18,800
Dental Assistants	14,500
Radiologic Technologists	8,600
Respiratory Therapy Workers	6,800
Dental Hygienists	6,300
Dentists	6,200
Operating Room Technicians	2,700
Dental Lab Technicians	2,600
Physical Therapy Assistants and Aides	2,400
Optometric Assistants	1,800
Veterinarians	1,450
Occupational Therapy Assistants	1,400
Chiropractors	1,200
Occupational Therapists	1,150
Electrocardiographic Technicians	1,000
Electroencephalographic Technicians	350

↓1

*Source: "Jobs with the brightest future," _Changing Times_, September 1977, pp. 6-11.

goals

Control M, R, and I keys.
☐ Type 70 strokes or more in 1 minute.

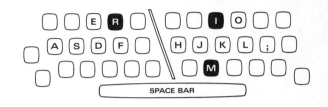

▶ **40-space line; single-space; each line three times or more; double-space between *different* lines.**

WARMUP

1 aaa sss dd ff jj kk lll ;;; hhh eee ooo

2 so; oak hoe joke ask folk old fade lead

M KEY

Use J finger.

3 jjj jmj mmm jjj jmj mmm jjj jmj mmm jmj

4 jmj mad mad jmj hem hem jmj jam jam jmj

5 alm alm me; me; mom mom ham ham ma; ma;

R KEY

Use F finger.

6 fff frf rrr fff frf rrr fff frf rrr frf

7 frf ore ore frf are are frf jar jar frf

8 ark ark mar mar arm arm ram ram red red

I KEY

Use K finger.

9 kkk kik iii kkk kik iii kkk kik iii kik

10 kik air air kik sir sir kik fir fir kik

11 hid hid is; is; ill ill did did dim dim

NEW KEY REINFORCEMENT

12 mmm mad mad mad mid mid mid ham ham ham

13 rrr rim rim rim ram ram ram rod rod rod

14 iii aim aim aim lie lie lie dim dim dim

15 home home firm firm hair hair mark mark

WORD PRACTICE

16 mod err farm see make irk form hem hide

17 loam fir dime lad film air mire sir lie

18 sham led made for idle rod ride so; far

19 mild ore dome elm hair ohm home are me;

70
74

goals

Type a complete research paper with a title page, table of contents, list of tables, and bibliography, from unarranged copy and notecards.

TYPING TIP
☐ Before you begin the research paper for Lessons 70–74, look over pages 130–136 for an overview of what you must do. Then plan what you think you should accomplish each day until you complete the paper. Allow time for proofreading, collating, and fastening the pages. Stick to your plan.

WARMUP

▶ Use Lesson 69 on page 128.

RESEARCH PAPER

▶ Type the first two pages of the research paper, shown on text pages 130 and 131. Use a 6-inch line and follow the spacing indicated. Make a carbon copy.

The miniature below was done in elite type.

SKILL CHECK

▶ For lessons 70–74, use the Skill Check on page 128.

A SURVEY OF CURRENT OCCUPATIONAL PROSPECTS

A Special Report

By (Your Name)

I. Purpose

One of the most important decisions that young people must make is what type of further training they will undertake after high school, or if they will seek further training at all. It is a very difficult decision to make, and it is often determined by the current occupational outlook. This paper will attempt to offer the results of findings concerning current occupational prospects for the future.

II. Research

Special government reports, periodicals, and recent textbooks were examined to determine the results of current surveys. A local survey was also conducted to determine if the national trends reported were in agreement with local trends.

III. Presentation of Data

The findings of this paper will be divided into seven general categories: health, scientific and technical, office, mechanics and repair, service, other good prospects, and less encouraging prospects.

20 ask for him; some of; has had; hear him
21 did he; did she; more of; see her home;
22 fall off; sale of; am here; he is here;
23 or else; if he is; as is; for he is ill;

SKILL CHECK

▶ Aim to type 70 strokes or more in 1 minute. Try it at least three times.

24 she made a film of his home; he did see
25 her farm; she makes a jade elk;

END-OF-PERIOD ROUTINE

Do you leave your work station in good order?

1. Remove your paper from the typewriter, using the paper release and pulling the bail forward or up.
2. Return the paper bail to the cylinder.
3. Center the carriage or carrier.
4. Turn off the machine if your typewriter is an electric machine.
5. Cover your machine if you are the last to use it for the day.
6. Put away all your supplies and leave your desk neat.

goals

Control T, N, and C keys. □ Type 80 strokes or more in 1 minute.

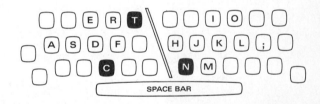

▶ 40-space line; single-space; each line three times or more; double-space between *different* lines.

1 asdf jkl; hj ed ik rf mj ol as df jk l;
2 jam has dad rim led elf oh; sad old oak

3 fff ftf ttt fff ftf ttt fff ftf ttt fff
4 ftf hat hat ftf jet jet ftf let let ftf
5 set set rat rat lot lot kit kit met met

RESEARCH PAPER

This project will take you several days to complete. You will be picking up a research paper at the point where all the research has been done. The paper has been organized and put in rough draft form. It is now your task to prepare a formal report from the pieces of information provided you.

▶ 69-1: MEMO

▶ Type this handwritten copy of a memo. Within the memo are specific directions for the completion of the rest of the project. Read the contents of the memo thoroughly before you type it. You may need to refer back to the section on memos for format.

Date: (Current Date)
To: Personal Typewriting Students
From: (Your Teacher's Name)
Subject: Special Typewriting Project

This project will take approximately five sessions to complete. ~~it.~~ In the project you will:

1. Read through the project completely before you begin to type it.
2. Collect all the materials that you will need for completing the project. ~~You will need~~ They include plain paper, carbon paper, some means of correcting errors, a pencil or pen, and some extra paper for calculating space.
3. ~~You are to~~ make one carbon copy of the paper.
4. ~~You may~~ choose whether to use footnotes or end notes. The information you need is on the library reference cards (pp. 133–134).
5. Type the paper so that it can be bound in a notebook.
6. Look up any information on spacing before you begin to type.

Now it's time to start the project. A good paper typed neatly and accurately will serve as a good model for other papers you may need to type in the future.

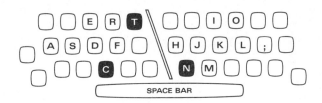

N KEY

Use J finger.

6 jjj jnj nnn jjj jnj nnn jjj jnj nnn jnj
7 jnj den den jnj son son jnj fan fan jnj
8 ton ton net net tan tan tin tin men men

C KEY

Use D finger.

9 ddd dcd ccc ddd dcd ccc ddd dcd ccc dcd
10 dcd cod cod dcd ace ace dcd can can dcd
11 car car con con doc doc arc arc cam cam

NEW KEY REINFORCEMENT

12 ttt tam tam tam ton ton ton cot cot cot
13 nnn not not not net net net man man man
14 ccc car car car con con con doc doc doc
15 care care cane cane tone tone cone cone

KEY JAMS

If you are using a typebar machine, the typebars may jam together. You should untangle them very carefully, one key at a time. Never yank or pull the typebars or the top of the keys.

You can prevent jamming the typebars by typing evenly and by stroking one key at a time.

▷ **40-space line; single space; each line three times or more; double-space between *different* lines.**

WORD PRACTICE

16 time sit irk jot arch nil join fit came
17 care aid one for coat ear dime ton name
18 note cam end cod loan ace fact act jest
19 more fat ten lot line the dome to; nice

PHRASE PRACTICE

20 to do; to see; to let; to take; to ask;
21 for her; for me; for the man; for home;
22 a joke; the fact; not more; make a hat;
23 are not here; has not; one kind; a jam;

SKILL CHECK

▷ See if you can type 80 strokes or more in 1 minute. Try it at least three times.

24 tell her that she can see him soon; the
25 jet can make it; find a kite for a lad;

goals

Type 34 wam for 5 minutes within 4 errors.
☐ Type a final draft of a memo from handwritten notes.

▶ 60-space line; single-space; each line three times; double-space between *different* lines.

WARMUP

1 Five or six more pages will be added to make a larger size.

2 Did you say '10, '29, '38, '47, or '56 is the correct year?

3 I hope that you can join us for a quiet outing by the lake.

Edit as you type.

4 What was the affect of the personal manager's first remark.
|1 |2 |3 |4 |5 |6 |7 |8 |9 |10 |11 |12

PREVIEW

▶ Practice these words before you take the Skill Check.

5 demonstrated illustrate relationship happiness quiver skill

6 William Tell, Kahlil Gibran, Cupid, Homer, archery, classic

7 Valentine's Day, Longfellow, Ulysses, famous, arrow, appear

SKILL CHECK

▶ Try to reach your goal of 34 words a minute with 4 errors or less.

8 The arrow from the archer's bow has been a subject for   12

9 many poems, stories, and songs down through the ages. When   24

10 you see the name William Tell you think about a man who was   36

11 an excellent marksman. He shot an apple off his son's head   48

12 with his bow and arrow. Kahlil Gibran used the bow and the   60

13 arrow to illustrate his concept of the relationship between   72

14 parent and child. Longfellow has used the bow and arrow as   84

15 part of many of his famous poems, and in a well-known Greek   96

16 classic by Homer, Ulysses amazed all of the suitors when he   108

17 demonstrated his mastery of the skill of archery. And last   120

18 of all, who can forget Cupid, who is always seen with a bow   132

19 and a quiver of arrows ready to shoot couples and make them   144

20 fall in love? Valentine's day is his time to appear and go   156

21 about his business of spreading happiness to as many people   168

22 as he can.   170
|1 |2 |3 |4 |5 |6 |7 |8 |9 |10 |11 |12 SI: 1.38

goals

Control right shift, V, and period keys. □ Type 90 strokes or more in 1 minute.

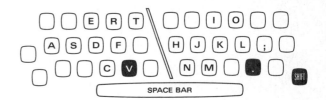

□ 40-space line; single-space; each line three times or more; double-space between *different* lines.

WARMUP

1 asdf jkl; hh ee oo rr ii mm ccc ttt nnn

2 act hen for oar rim jar kid sir lee as;

RIGHT SHIFT KEY

Use Semicolon finger.

Use the right shift key to capitalize letters typed by the left hand. Keep your J finger in place. *Reach* with your semicolon finger and hold the right shift key down. *Strike* the letter to be capitalized. *Release* the right shift key and bring your semicolon finger back to home position.

3 ;;; A;; A;; ;;; S;; S;; ;;; D;; D;; ;;;

4 ;;; Sam Sam ;;; Don Don ;;; Ann Ann ;;;

5 ;;; Flo Flo ;;; Dot Dot ;;; Cal Cal ;;;

V KEY

Use F finger.

6 fff fvf vvv fff fvf vvv fff fvf vvv fff

7 fvf vet vet fvf via via fvf vie vie fvf

8 Vel Vel Eva Eva Van Van Vic Vic Val Val

Remember to (a) *reach,* (b) *strike,* and (c) *release* when you capitalize a letter.

. KEY

Use L finger.

9 lll l.l ... lll l.l ... lll l.l ... lll

10 l.l St. St. l.l Rd. Rd. l.l Dr. Dr. l.l

11 l.l Ct. Ct. l.l Fr. Fr. l.l Tr. Tr. l.l

NEW KEY REINFORCEMENT

Space *once* after a period when it follows an abbreviation within a sentence. Space *twice* after a period at the end of a sentence.

12 Dr. Tai took a jet to Erie to see Anne.

13 She has a home on Elm St. She is nice.

14 Rahn Rd. is the site. Val can send it.

15 Al left his car here. Eve is her name.

The data in Table 2 show the percentage of graduating students who had taken one or more semesters of typing in three different percentage groups. The average of the 20 schools gives an approximate 85 percent of the combined graduating seniors in all schools as the number who had taken a formal course in typing. This finding is almost identical with the results found by James in his study.

Table 2

Percent of Graduating Seniors Who Have Had Typing

Percentage Category	Number of Schools	Percent of Schools
90–100	5	25
80–89	10	50
70–79	5	25

The data from this study show that typing is taken today by a very large percentage of high school students. As someone has said, "Typing is considered more and more as a tool of literacy."

Remember: 6–8 blank lines at the bottom of the page.

OPTIONAL PROJECT

▶ Type the report in bound form. Select another placement style for reference notes.

COMPOSING

▶ **Now that you know how a term paper or formal report is typed and you know something about the content of a formal report, try your hand at composing a paper which will be typed as a formal report, either bound or unbound.**

Your report is to be on the subject of letter styles (the spacing within a letter, the parts of a letter, etc.) and how to type various styles in proper form. Compose an introduction to your paper and then, using one or two tables, explain to the reader of the paper the proper way to type business and personal letters. Perhaps you will type one or two letters to illustrate how a personal letter differs from a business letter. You may want to go back to Unit 6 to review letter styles. The placement chart for letters is in Lesson 44. You will want to *outline, draft, edit,* and then *type* your formal report.

40-space line; single space; each line three times or more; double-space between *different* lines.

WORD PRACTICE

16 ask her are dim fee vat old foe red oak
17 via jar for van his hat tin mid cot elf
18 rime mare tone Rome more same Erie vine
19 like side fine arch make some tear dike

PHRASE PRACTICE

20 to the; so that it; if not; as fine as;
21 she is not; in that; of the; more than;
22 has not had; join in; a lot of; for it;
23 make a joke; via air; take care; it is;

SENTENCE PRACTICE

24 Ted and Arch sold him the last red oak.
25 Val can find some old jam jars to sell.
26 Rod and Sam hit the dot on the tin can.
27 Dick and Fred read the end of the tale.

COUNTING ERRORS

It is not surprising if you make errors—you may average about two per line at this point. They are signals to help you know what you need to practice. The following illustration will show you how to mark and count your errors.

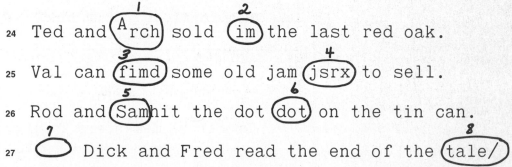

24 Ted and Arch sold im the last red oak.

25 Val can fimd some old jam jsrx to sell.

26 Rod and Samhit the dot dot on the tin can.

27 Dick and Fred read the end of the tale/

Count as one error and circle each word:

1. With an incomplete capital or a raised capital.
2. With a stroke that does not show.
3. With one wrong letter.
4. With more than one wrong letter.
5. Preceding an error in spacing.
6. That is repeated or omitted.
7. With wrong indention, alignment, or spacing.
8. Preceding an error in punctuation.

determine the percentage of graduating seniors who had
taken one or more semesters of typing.

Table 1 presents the data indicating the number of
semesters of typing offered in the 20 high schools.
Only 3 of the 20 schools, 15 percent, offer one semester of typing; the remaining 17 schools have two or
more semesters in the curriculum. The 3 schools that
have only one semester of typing are among the smallest
in the study; furthermore, they are schools with strong
academic programs and typing is offered only for personal use. There were 7 other schools in the study
that reported having a one-semester personal use course
in typing in addition to the longer-length program.
The schools offering four semesters of typing also have
strong vocational programs, apart from a course in personal typing.

Leave 1 to 3 blank lines
to separate the table from
the text.

Table 1 ↓2

Number of Semesters Typing is Offered ↓3

Number of Semesters	Number of Schools	Percent of Schools ↓2
1	3	15
2	6	30
4	11	55

FIGURING NUMBER OF WORDS TYPED IN A MINUTE (wam)

To find how many *average* words you type in the time allowed, count every 5 strokes as 1 average word. A 40-stroke line is 8 words long; two such lines count as 16 words. For an incomplete line, use the scale: if you stop above a number, that number is your word count. If you stop between numbers, the number to the left of the last letter that you typed is your word count.

Example: If you type lines 28, 29, and 30 below and start over, getting as far as the word *can* in line 28, you've typed 18 + 2 = 20 words; *can* counts as 2 because it is in the second word group—a fraction counts as a whole word.

Total words per line is shown in this far column. ↓

SKILL CHECK

▶ Aim to type 18 words or more in 1 minute. Try it at least three times. Circle your errors too.

```
28  Vic can make a kite sail in the air and        8

29  come to rest on the hill.  Ed joins him        16

30  near Fred.                                      18
   |1    |2    |3    |4    |5    |6    |7    |8
```

goals

Control W, comma, and G keys. □ Type 20 words or more in 1 minute.

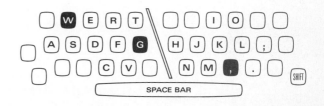

▶ 40-space line; single space; each line three times or more; double-space between *different* lines.

WARMUP

```
1  asdf jkl; cc ii vv oo rr mm tt nn ee hh

2  ate for kit mar con van lot sit hid jot
```

W KEY

Use S finger.

```
3  sss sws www sss sws www sss sws www sws

4  sws law law sws mow mow sws vow vow sws

5  how how jaw jaw now now low low mew mew
```

, KEY

Use K finger.

```
6  kkk k,k ,,, kkk k,k ,,, kkk k,k ,,, k,k

7  k,k in, in, k,k me, me, k,k an, an, k,k

8  so, so, he, he, we, we, do, do, la, la,
```

TYPING CLASSES IN TWENTY HIGH SCHOOLS ↓3

UNBOUND MANUSCRIPT WITH FOOTNOTES

▷ 6-inch line; tabs at 5 and center; double spacing.

This is a report of a study to determine the extent to which typing is included in the curricular offerings of 20 selected high schools in the western part of the country. The study was conducted by the members of a personal typing class in one of the high schools under the supervision of Miss Susan Paul, the instructor of that class. The schools selected were those in which the typing teacher was a classmate of Miss Paul in her teacher preparation program at the Atwell State University.

The number of students taking typing in high school has greatly increased in recent years. A study of 58 selected high schools in the Midwest[1] found that in 1952 only 62 percent of the graduating seniors had taken one or more semesters of typing. In 1977 an average of reports from these same schools showed that there had been an increase to 84 percent of the graduates who had taken typing that year.

This report of the survey of 20 high schools had two objectives: to determine the number of semesters of typing offered in each of the high schools, and to

↓1 _____

↓2

1. R. M. James, "A Study of the Extent to Which Typing is Offered in High Schools in 1977 as Compared to 1952," unpublished master's thesis, Atwell State University, 1978.

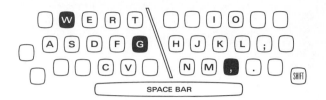

G KEY

Use F finger.

9 fff fgf ggg fff fgf ggg fff fgf ggg fff
10 fgf nag nag fgf cog cog fgf rig rig fgf
11 fig fig leg leg jag jag wig wig log log

NEW KEY REINFORCEMENT

12 www wit wit wit tow tow tow won won won
13 ,,, of, of, of, to, to, to, he, he, he,
14 ggg gal gal gal tag tag tag got got got
15 flag flag grow grow crow crow lag, lag,

WORD PRACTICE

16 win keg fig dew dog and maw dog tow wig
17 age mow fin ohm lid gin car jet vie row
18 wind gone flog wide game went girl wife
19 done hike same long wilt gild cove sent

PHRASE PRACTICE

20 for the, was not, go for, had to, at a;
21 now for me, did not get, can have some;
22 will see; near here; too low; for more;
23 to the sea; did not ask; as far as the;

SKILL CHECK

▷ Aim to type 20 words or more in 1 minute. Try it at least three times. Don't forget to circle your errors.

24 Val likes to fish and she also likes to   8
25 jog. When it is raining, she can see a   16
26 movie or do chores.   20
    |1 |2 |3 |4 |5 |6 |7 |8

CLINICS

At the end of each of the four units in Part One, you will find a *clinic*. The clinic may help you pinpoint trouble spots and give you a clue to where you might need addi- tional practice. It may show you particular strengths in your typing skill. It may also be used simply as a review of what you have learned thus far.

goals

Type 33 wam on a 5-minute timing. ☐ Type a formal manuscript with tables.

WARMUP

Insert the correct punctuation where you see ___.

1 Both sexes can acquire the agility to jump and run quickly.

2 Bad posture at the machine can initiate some typing errors.

3 I ordered #1408 on April 2, but you sent #2408 on April 21.

4 Look at Belinda__the girl in blue__return that tennis ball.

|1 |2 |3 |4 |5 |6 |7 |8 |9 |10 |11 |12

SKILL CHECK

▶ Try to type 33 words a minute in a 5-minute timing with 4 or fewer errors.

5   Let us talk about sports--sports in general. Physical   12

6 skill and strength, an alert mind, zest, vigor, and purpose   24

7 are all essential for a person to succeed as an athlete. A   36

8 person who wants to take part in an athletic event, whether   48

9 amateur or professional, needs to practice at least several   60

10 hours each day. This is what it takes to compete.   70

11   Friendships are formed through sports. The ability of   82

12 persons to get along with one another is very important for   94

13 sports we compete in. It is very easy to see that feelings   106

14 are strong when experts vie for trophies and strive to gain   118

15 honors for groups they represent. Such tests of friendship   130

16 often bring out good qualities in people which they did not   142

17 realize were in them. People who are well adjusted can win   154

18 without gloating and can lose without becoming bitter.   165

|1 |2 |3 |4 |5 |6 |7 |8 |9 |10 |11 |12 **SI: 1.43**

FORMAL REPORT

The manuscript on the following pages will permit you to type a formal report in unbound form. Remember what you have learned so far about typing a formal paper—you must have a bottom margin of at least one inch (6 blank lines) on *each* page; begin typing on line 13 on the first page only; begin typing on line 7 for all pages *after* page 1.

While the data reported in the study are fictitious, they are accurate in indicating the high numbers of students who do take a course in typing before graduation.

goals

Analyze key control and practice remedial drills to strengthen weakest controls. □ Type 20 words in 1 minute.

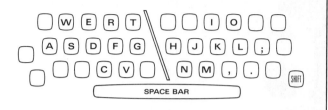

▶ **40-space line; single space; each line three times or more; double-space between *different* lines.**

TWO CLINIC ROUTINES

Two suggested routines for the clinic are outlined below. Use one or the other, depending upon the time you will spend on the clinic.

20-Minute Activity
Skill Check: 1 copy
Drills: odd-numbered lines once; even-numbered lines twice
Skill Check: 2 tries or until goal is reached

40-Minute Activity
Skill Check: 3 copies
Drills: odd-numbered lines twice; even-numbered lines three times
Skill Check: 4 tries or until goal is achieved

SKILL CHECK
▶ Aim to improve your control of the keys. Try to type 20 words in 1 minute.

1 ask ask lad lad dad dad fad fad sad sad
2 ask a lad; ask a dad; a fad; a sad lad;
3 lass lass jade jade half half fall fall
4 ask a lass; a fall; a jade; half a safe

5 hoe hoe seal seal joke joke a lot a lot
6 has a hoe; see a seal; a joke; a lot of
7 keel keel hole hole lake lake feel feel
8 has a keel; feel sod; see hole; a lake;

9 maid maid some some lime lime dear dear
10 a maid did; had some; a lime; dear sir;
11 mile mile more more lore lore like like
12 a mile; more foes; hear a line; like it

13 thin thin that that cold cold one, one,
14 the thin log, that cold one, no one can
15 call call can, can, man, man, lake lake
16 call on me, if he can, man at the lake,

17 lake clear, calm near, the edge, clear,
18 A lake is clear and calm near the edge.
19 water, water, five, five, center center
20 The water is five feet near the center.

21 Dick and Cal can swim in five feet when   8
22 the water is still. Ted will join them   16
23 if he can get there.   20

|1 |2 |3 |4 |5 |6 |7 |8

Protecting Your work. If the original copy of a term paper or research report is
lost, one has the carbon to avoid spending hours of extra time collecting
the information again and rewriting the report. In the event that something happens to the original (and the possibility of something happening
to an original is always a definite hazard), the carbon provides an exact
copy.[1] Reports handed into an instructor may become lost on occasion.
Another good reason to make a carbon copy is ~~that you always~~ to have it for
reference in the original way it was written. Your instructor may write
notes and make corrections on the original copy; by having the carbon copy
on hand you can easily compare the two copies to see ~~to see~~ what revisions
were made and why.

Correcting the Carbon Copy. Many people ~~in making the original copy~~
are not particular about making corrections on ~~the~~ a carbon copy since it serves
only informational purposes. In fact, some offices do not require corrections to be noted on a file carbon copy unless a number of them are
involved. This may be all right if the correction is not an important
one, but a careful check should be made to make certain of this. Amounts, dates, and other facts
should be corrected on the carbon as they alter the content in a signficant
way.

_____

1. There are records of students who have spent years working on
Ph.D. dissertations only to have the dissertation ruined by fire or theft.
The lack of a carbon copy in these instances has tragic results.

The footnote in this report gives additional information to the reader.

goals

Control B, U, and left shift keys. ☐ Type 15 wam for 2 minutes within 4 errors.

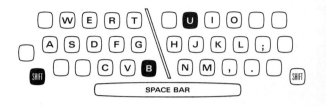

▷ **40-space line; single-space; each line three times or more; double-space between *different* lines.**

WARMUP

1 aaa sss dd ff jj kk lll ;;; www ggg ,,,
2 mad mad van van wig wig cot cot her her
3 Tom; Tom; Ann; Ann; Sam; Sam; Dot; Dot;

B KEY

Use F finger.

4 fff fbf bbb fff fbf bbb fff fbf bbb fbf
5 fbf fib fib fbf bad bad fbf job job fbf
6 bend bend fb bill bill fb boar boar fbf

U KEY

Use J finger.

7 jjj juj uuu jjj juj uuu jjj juj uuu juj
8 juj dug dug juj use use juj lug lug juj
9 tuck tuck ju undo undo ju used used juj

LEFT SHIFT KEY

Use A finger.

Keep your F finger in place; *reach* with your A finger and hold the left shift key down. Now *strike* the letter to be capitalized. *Release* the left shift key and bring your left hand back to home position.

10 fff Jff Jff ddd Kdd Kdd sss Lss Lss aaa
11 aaa Hal Hal aaa Mad Mad aaa aaa Lea Lea
12 Jeff Jeff Ki Kidd Kidd La Lass Lass Mr.
13 Hans Hans Jean Jean King King Lori Lori

Remember to (a) *reach,* (b) *strike,* and (c) *release* when you want to capitalize a letter.

NEW KEY REINFORCEMENT

14 bbb bat bat bat beg beg beg bit bit bit
15 uuu tub tub tub fun fun fun us, us, us,
16 JJJ Jim Jim KKK Ken Ken LLL Len Len aaa

TO MAKE A CARBON COPY place the shiny side of the carbon sheet against the paper on which the carbon is to be made. Straighten sides and top of carbon pack before inserting it into your machine. Hold the pack with your left hand; turn the cylinder with your right hand.

BOUND REPORT. You may wish to place your typed report in a binder of some kind. If you do, you will need to allow a wider left margin for the binding. Leave 1½ inches for the left margin and 1 inch for the right. You will need to find a new center point and margin stops—move margins and tab stops 3 spaces to the right.

CARBONS ↓13

A Report by Clara O'Brien

Introduction

Traditionally, whenever a copy of a letter was *needed* ~~to be made~~ for the file~~s copy~~ or to send to a thrid person, the method of *preparing* ~~making~~ that copy was with the use of carbon paper. In recent years, however, much of the duplicating of ~~the original~~ letter*s*, manuscript*s*, or other material has been done through the process of photocopy machines. Omitting carbons makes typing much easier and faster. *Furthermore,* ~~The~~ copy machine gives an accurate reproduction of the original letter with letterhead and other information that might be printed on the original *but* ~~and~~ would not be shown on a carbon copy.

Despite the advantages of photocopying, ~~however,~~ a need still remains for carbon copies in the office. Many offices still have thier file copies made from carbon because *this method* ~~it is~~ cheaper or more convenient ~~or because they may not have the copy equipment.~~ ~~Many companies provide~~ *They may purchase* "preassembled" snap-out carbon packs in which sheets of carbon paper are interleaved between sheets of copy paper. ↓3

Personal-Use Copies

Carbon paper is convenient for personal typing. In preparing *(type)* any of report for a high school class or perhaps a longer term paper in college work, it is strongly recommended that a file copy be made using carbon paper.

17 bbb iii bib bib bid bid bit bit bin bin
18 uuu ggg dug dug mug mug lug lug jug jug
19 mmm ,,, em, em, am, am, rim, rim, room,
20 www aaa war war wan wan was was wag wag

KEY LOCATION PRACTICE

Try to remember the location of all the letter keys you have learned thus far.

21 back back dark dark buck buck hark hark
22 saga saga rags rags task task fast fast
23 name name gain gain band band wane wane
24 live live over over jolt jolt joke joke

SENTENCE PRACTICE

25 The brownish shirt looks nice on Louis.
26 Fads come or go but this one will lose.
27 Move the desk and cots to the new room.
28 A goat, a boar, and a cow feed on corn.
  |1 |2 |3 |4 |5 |6 |7 |8

SKILL CHECK

▶ Copy twice in 2 minutes within 4 errors (15 wam for 2 minutes).

29 The ice sled race, just over, was great   8
30 fun. Kathie and Ben came in first.   15
  |1 |2 |3 |4 |5 |6 |7 |8

goals

Control P, Q, and colon keys. □ Type 16 wam for 2 minutes within 4 errors.

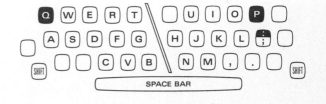

▶ **40-space line; single-space; each line three times or more; double-space between *different* lines.**

WARMUP

1 a;sldkfjgh a;sldkfjgh a;sldkfjgh a;sldk
2 tan tan bow bow fit fit ask ask Mr. Mr.
3 Jack Jack Sue; Sue; veal veal that that

goals

Type 32 wam on a 5-minute timing. □ Type a formal report with carbon copy. □ Type a formal report in bound form and unbound form. □ Type from rough-draft copy.

TYPING TIP
□ Use a dash to show an abrupt break in thought or to set off an afterthought.

Here's gourmet food in a jiffy—economical too!

I believe she said the convention would be held in Portland, Oregon—or was it Portland, Maine?

WARMUP

Insert the correct punctuation where you see ___.

1 With quick reflexes and a quick mind, you can win the game.

2 In a term paper, the table of contents page is numbered ii.

3 The 8 members of the squad should report at 5 or 7 o'clock.

4 We went sailing on Whitewater Lake last fall__it was great!

|1 |2 |3 |4 |5 |6 |7 |8 |9 |10 |11 |12

SKILL CHECK

▶ Try to type 32 words a minute in a 5-minute timing with 4 or fewer errors.

5   No doubt sports is next to weather as the most debated   12

6 and talked about subject. A close game arouses emotions of   24

7 people who seldom get ruffled. Everyone gets into the act.   36

8 A forthcoming game always produces much discussion and then   48

9 the postmortem, the replaying of the game, causes even more   60

10 talk. If the home team wins, the excitement of the winning   72

11 goal, touchdown, basket, home run, or serve, is the subject   84

12 of many lively discussions in the days following that game.   96

13   An indication of the wide appeal of sports can be seen   108

14 through the quantity of reading space devoted to the matter   120

15 by both the newspapers and magazines. Television and radio   132

16 spend hundreds of minutes during each week to show and tell   134

17 the fan about the next game and/or the game just completed.   156

18 What a great topic!   160

|1 |2 |3 |4 |5 |6 |7 |8 |9 |10 |11 |12 **SI: 1.44**

P KEY Use Sem finger.	4 ;;; ;p; ppp ;;; ;p; ppp ;;; ;p; ppp ;p; 5 ;p; pan pan ;p; ape ape ;p; apt apt ;p; 6 deep deep ;p wasp wasp ;p poor poor ;p;
Q KEY Use A finger.	7 aaa aqa qqq aaa aqa qqq aaa aqa qqq aqa 8 aqa quit quit aq quad quad aq quip quip 9 equal equal quest quest quota quota aqa
: KEY Use left shift and Sem finger.	10 ;;; ;:; ::: ;;; ;:; ::: ;;; ;:; ::: ;:; 11 ;:; Dr. Bua: ;:; Mrs. Ott: ;:; To Jo: 12 Ms. Aps: Ms. Win: Dear Edna: Margie:
NEW KEY REINFORCEMENT	13 aqua aqua quite quite quo quo quid quid 14 per per paw paw pot pot map map ape ape 15 ;:; ;:; to: to: re: re: Jo: Jo: :
WORD PATTERNS	16 anan anti anti band band scan scan plan 17 lolo lone lone blow blow polo polo lore 18 titi tied tied stir stir anti anti time 19 papa pale pale span span papa papa opal
PHRASE PRACTICE	20 is our, is our, He is, He is, will quit 21 are too long, are too long, is just new 22 Keep in, Keep in, or run, small poodle.
SENTENCE PRACTICE	23 King is our dog. He is a small poodle. 24 Pam will quit. The hours are too long. 25 His skateboard is blue; it is just new. 26 Walk, jog, jump, or run. Keep in form. |1 |2 |3 |4 |5 |6 |7 |8

ANALYZING YOUR STROKING PROBLEMS

Compare your typing of sentence 26 above with the examples on the next page to analyze your stroking problems and to learn what to do about them.

All pages of manuscript *after* page 1 begin with the page number on line 7, the body on line 10.

2. *Reference Notes.* Many journals and textbooks now place the references within the running text.[3] References are identified at the appropriate place in the body of the manuscript by enclosing in parentheses the author's surname, year of publication, and page reference. A reader interested in more information on an idea or quotation may look at the bibliography at the end of the manuscript.

Meaning of Terms

Certain abbreviations may be utilized when typing footnotes. When a footnote refers to a work that was fully identified in the footnote *immediately* preceding, it may be shortened to "Ibid."[4] When a footnote refers to a work identified in an earlier but not immediately preceding note, just state the author or authors' last names and the new page number. If a footnote requires identifying three or more authors, list only the first author's name and use "et al." to represent the other names. "Et al." means "and others."

▶ Type this NOTES page for problem 1 only.

↓13
NOTES
↓3

1. Alan C. Lloyd and Russell J. Hosler, *Personal Typing,* 3d ed., McGraw-Hill, New York, 1969, p. 116.

2. William A. Sabin, *The Gregg Reference Manual,* 5th ed., McGraw-Hill, New York, 1977, p. 278.

3. William L. Powell, "Provide Referencing Choices in Teaching Manuscript Typing," *NBEA Forum,* October, 1976, p. 25.

4. Sabin, p. 285.

▶ Type a bibliography page and make two copies to use as the last page for all three problems. See pages 103–104 for information on typing bibliographies.

Separate a footnote from the text above it by a 2-inch line of underscores (20 pica spaces or 24 elite spaces). Be sure to double-space after typing the line in order that a blank space will separate the line and the first footnote below the line.[1]

Footnotes may instead be grouped together in a section at the end of the manuscript or report. "This style is becoming increasingly popular because it is much easier to type than the foot-of-the-page style."[2]

---

1. Alan C. Lloyd and Russell J. Hosler, Personal Typing, 3d ed., McGraw-Hill Book Company, New York, 1969, p. 116.

2. William A. Sabin, The Gregg Reference Manual, 5th ed., McGraw-Hill, New York, 1977, p. 278.

▶ **Use this example of footnotes for Problem 2.**

Separate a footnote from the text above it by a 2-inch line of underscores (20 pica spaces or 24 elite spaces). Be sure to double-space after typing the line in order that a blank space will separate the line and the first footnote below the line. (Lloyd & Hosler, 1969, p. 116)

Footnotes may instead be grouped together in a section at the end of the manuscript or report. "This style is becoming increasingly popular because it is much easier to type than the foot-of-the-page style." (Sabin, 1977, p. 278) If you adopt this style, use a fresh page at the end of the report; space down 13 and type NOTES.

▶ **Use this example of reference notes for Problem 3.**

USING:	IF YOUR WORK LOOKS LIKE THIS:	THIS IS WHAT YOU ARE DOING:
A typebar or an element machine,	Walk, jog, jump, or run. Keep in form. Walk, jog, jump, ot run. Keep in form.	You're typing with crisp, even, *good* strokes. Don't worry about errors for the present.
A typebar machine,	Walk, jog, jump, or run. Keep in form. Walk, jog, jump, or run. Keep im form.	You're *pushing* keys, holding them down. You should peck keys, release them quickly.
A typebar or an element machine,	Walk, jump, or or run. Kep in form. Wlk, jump, or run or jog. Keep in form.	You looked away from your copy (and lost the place)! You omitted or repeated words.
A typebar or an element machine,	Walk, jog, jump, or run. Keepin form. Walk, jog, jump, or run. Keep in form.	You're typing in sudden spurts instead of in smooth rhythm.
A typebar machine,	Walk, jog, jump, or run. Keep in form. Walk, jog, jump, or run. Keep in form.	Get some iron into your fingers! You're typing much too lightly. Snap keys firmly.
A typebar or an element machine,	Wa lk, jog, jum p, or run. Keep i n form. W alk, j og, jump ,or run. Keepi n form.	You're letting your thumb rest on the space bar. Keep the thumb a half inch above it.
A typebar or an element machine,	Walk,jog, jump or run. Keepin form. Walk, jog,jump or run. Keepi nform.	You're forgetting to space after words. Say the word "space" to yourself after each word.

SKILL CHECK

▶ Try to type 16 wam for 2 minutes within 4 errors.

27	Dear Jo: Since we talked last evening,	8
28	I saw Pat. She has agreed to work with	16
29	us on our design if it will not require	24
30	too much time. That is good news. Bob	32

|1 |2 |3 |4 |5 |6 |7 |8

goals

Control hyphen, Z, and diagonal keys. □ Type 17 wam for 2 minutes within 4 errors.

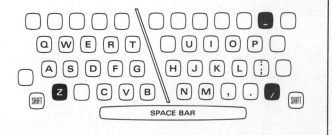

▶ 40-space line; single-space; each line three times or more; double-space between *different* lines.

WARMUP

1 a;sldkfjgh a;sldkfjgh a;sldkfjgh a;sldk

2 Nat Nat tip tip end end but but ire ire

3 veto gull blow ajar glue quip dash Dick

REPORTS

A long report (over one page) is typed on a 6-inch line (60-pica or 70-elite spaces) with the body double-spaced. The first page begins on line 13. All other pages begin on line 7, where the page number is typed. The text begins on line 10. *Be careful* in typing as each page must have 6–8 blank lines in the bottom margin. If you need to break a paragraph, at least 2 lines should be typed on the first page and 2 lines on the following page. *Hint*—before inserting your paper, draw a very light pencil mark at the right edge of your paper, about 2 inches from the bottom, as a signal that you are nearing the end of the paper. Erase the mark when you finish typing the page.

MANUSCRIPT TYPING

▶ **Read the complete report before you type it.**

PROBLEM 1.

▶ **6-inch line; tabs at 5, 10, center; double spacing. Type the manuscript, with a separate page for footnotes and a bibliography page.**

PROBLEM 2.

▶ **Same as Problem 1, except place footnotes at the bottom of the page.**

PROBLEM 3.

▶ **Same as Problem 1, except insert reference notes.**

A long quotation (4 or more typed lines) should be single-spaced and indented 5 spaces on each side.

A quote of 3 or fewer typed lines is shown in quotation marks.

Remember: 6–8 blank lines at bottom.

FOOTNOTES AND REFERENCE NOTES ↓2

A Report by John R. Russell ↓3

This report will discuss the purpose and the placement of footnotes and reference notes as they are used in formal writing. ↓3

Purposes of Footnotes and Reference Notes

Footnotes may be used to provide a further explanation to the reader of a point in the text, or they may be used to identify the source of material mentioned or quoted in the text. Reference notes direct the reader to the bibliography, where the source is identified fully.

Placement of Footnotes and Reference Notes

1. *Footnotes.* The footnote may appear at the bottom of the page. When this method is used, each footnote is a numbered, single-spaced paragraph with the first line indented. A footnote must be separated from the body of a report. One book states:

> Separate a footnote from the text above it by a 2-inch line of underscores (20 pica spaces or 24 elite spaces). Be sure to double-space after typing the line in order that a blank space will separate the line and the first footnote below the line.[1]

Footnotes may instead be grouped together in a section at the end of the manuscript or report. "This style is becoming increasingly popular because it is much easier to type than the foot-of-the-page style."[2] If you adopt this style, use a fresh page at the end of the report; space down 13 and type NOTES. Space down 3 to begin typing the references in the same order as they were cited within the text. Indent the first line of each note 5 spaces.

■ (hyphen) KEY

Use Sem finger.

Keep your J finger close to home position as you reach upward.

Z KEY

Use A finger.

Keep your F finger in home position as you reach down.

■ (diagonal) KEY

Use Sem finger.

Keep your J finger in home position as you reach down.

NEW KEY REINFORCEMENT

WORD PATTERNS

PHRASE PRACTICE

SENTENCE PRACTICE

4 ;;; ;p— ;—; ——— ;;; ;p— ;—; ——— ;p— ;—;
5 ;p—; ;p—; one-third blue-green two-step
6 ;— great-aunt ;— first-hand ;— one-half

7 aaa aza zzz aaa aza zzz aaa aza zzz aza
8 aza zap zap aza zoo zoo aza aza zag aza
9 zone zone az zeal zeal az quiz quiz aza

10 ;;; ;/; /// ;;; ;/; /// ;;; ;/; /// ;/;
11 ;/; r/c r/c ;/; c/o c/o ;/; ;/; a/c ;/;
12 his/hers his/hers ;/; she/he she/he ;/;

13 quick-frozen; up-to-date; double-spaced
14 az zip zip zip zig zig zig zero zero az
15 and/or and/or pro/con pro/con n/c n/c /

16 iziz size size whiz whiz quiz quiz fizz
17 ququ quip quip quit quit aqua aqua quad
18 wewe wear wear owed owed awed awed weak
19 vivi visa visa avid avid evil evil view
20 MaMa Mark Mark Marg Marg Marj Marj Matt

21 when the, when the, has been has been,
22 have had, have had, that was, that was,
23 first one, first one, of them, of them,
24 could use, could use, a/c d/c, a/c d/c,

25 Please send the goods to him via truck.
26 Tim saw the zebra as he toured the zoo.
27 One-fifth of the total was sold to her.
28 One could use both a/c and d/c current.

|1 |2 |3 |4 |5 |6 |7 |8

goals

Type 32 wam on a 5-minute timing. ☐ Type a 2-page formal report with footnotes and reference notes. ☐ Learn reference terminology.

TYPING TIP
☐ Do not capitalize after a colon if the material cannot stand alone as a sentence.

Two courses are required: typing and English.

▶ **60-space line; single-space; each line three times or more or as many times as you can in a minute. Time permitting, do extra copies of whichever line best fits your practice needs. Use these same directions for each one of the Warmup drills in Unit 11.**

WARMUP

Insert the correct punctuation where you see ___.

1 The low haze gave a picturesque beauty to the morning view.

2 Typing skills will get you a job for the rest of your life.

3 Our Chapter No. 1522 was chartered in 1947 with 7 students.

4 I can suggest two skills for everyone__typing and English.

|1 |2 |3 |4 |5 |6 |7 |8 |9 |10 |11

SKILL CHECK

▶ **Try to type 32 words a minute in a 5-minute timing with 4 or fewer errors.**

5   How about a game of ball in your backyard sandlot on a   12

6 warm summer's day? Or what about a game to be played under   24

7 the starry, hazy sky of a hot summer's evening, a game that   36

8 will excite a crowd into yells and applause for the winning   48

9 team? All this can be true in the game of softball. Liked   60

10 at all ages, by both sexes, it is a game that appears to be   72

11 for all Americans. Many students enjoy games between rival   84

12 school teams. In later years, employees may form a team to   96

13 compete with teams from assorted other firms in their area.   108

14   Because equipment needs are very moderate, the game is   120

15 available for enjoyment by almost anyone who wishes to play   132

16 it. The ball used to play the game may vary from a 12-inch   144

17 size to a 16-inch size. The larger size is most often used   156

18 in an amateur game.   160

|1 |2 |3 |4 |5 |6 |7 |8 |9 |10 |11 |12 **SI: 1.35**

USES OF THE HYPHEN

1. Construct the dash by striking the hyphen key *twice*. Do not leave any space before or after a dash.

   ```
   Money--that is all he thinks about.
   ```

2. Use the hyphen to indicate that a word is divided.

   ```
   We will draw a new plan for this proj-
   ect.
   ```

3. Use the hyphen to tie compound words together.

   ```
   A social was held for the senator-elect
   and his runner-up.
   ```

4. Hyphenate phrases used as compound adjectives before a noun.

   ```
   A question-and-answer period followed the
   talk.
   ```

SKILL CHECK

▷ Try to type 17 wam or more for 2 minutes within 4 errors.

```
29  The hot spell must break--it lingers on       8
30  forever.  While some might rejoice with      16
31  laugh-filled picnics in the sun, others      24
32  with quiet zeal wait for rains to renew      32
33  the world.                                   34
    |1     |2     |3     |4     |5     |6     |7     |8
```

10 goals

Control Y, X, and ? keys.
☐ Type 18 wam for 2 minutes within 4 errors.

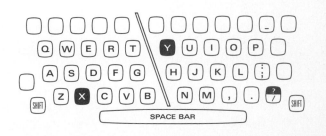

▷ **40-space line; single-space; each line three times or more; double-space between *different* lines.**

WARMUP

```
1  a;-;sldkfjgh a;/;sldkfjgh a;sl.ldk,fjgh
2  evil evil oboe oboe peck peck rink rink
3  quit quit maze maze high high pawn pawn
```

Y KEY

Use J finger.

```
4  jjj jyj yyy jjj jyj yyy jjj jyj yyy jyj
5  jyj joy joy jyj yes yes jyj yet yet jyj
6  obey obey jy myth myth jy yard yard jyj
```

62 goals

Strengthen composing skill by writing a set of directions and typing them in an acceptable format.
☐ Write a set of steps on "how to do" something.

WARMUP

▶ **62-1. Choose a local park for an outing and write a set of driving directions. Use the example to help you compose them.**

Remember to: outline, draft, edit, and retype.

Typing Hint: To make lines (underscores) at odd and vertical angles, loosen the paper (paper release) and turn the paper gently to the angle that you want.

▶ **62-2. Using the numbered list in Task 62-1 as an example, compose a one-page enumerated paper on "how to do" something. Be creative! Describe how to build a snowman, or how to climb a tree, or how to surf or . . . .**

Remember to: outline, draft, edit, retype.

SKILL CHECK

▶ **Use the Skill Check from Lesson 61, p. 116.**

▶ **Use lines 1–4 of Lesson 61 on page 116.**

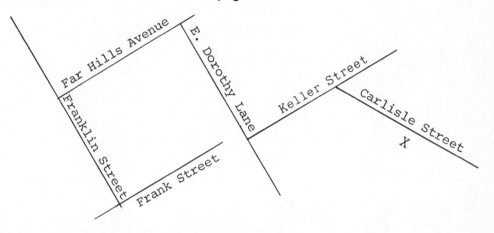

DRIVING DIRECTIONS
To Monte Villa Recreation Center
1284 Carlisle Street

1. Leave the high school by Frank Street exit and turn <u>left</u> on Franklin Street.

2. Go four blocks passing a church on the right and a nursery school on the left. Turn <u>right</u> at the traffic light on to Far Hills Avenue.

3. Follow Far Hills Avenue for about one mile passing a bank on the right, a MacDonald's restaurant on the left, and a large shopping center on the left. Turn <u>right</u> on East Dorothy Lane and stay in the <u>left</u> lane.

4. Proceed on East Dorothy Lane staying in the <u>left</u> lane. Go five blocks and turn <u>left</u> on Keller Street.

5. Go two blocks on Keller Street and turn <u>right</u> on to Carlisle Street. The Monte Villa Recreation Center is a block and a half down on the right side of the street. There is a large parking lot in the rear of the center. See you there!

7 sss sxs xxx sss sxs xxx sss sxs xxx sxs

8 sxs axe axe sxs box box sxs six six sxs

9 oxen oxen Sioux Sioux next next tax tax

10 ;;; ;?; ??? ;`;; ;?; ??? ;;; ;?; ??? ;?;

11 who? who? ;?; what? what? ;?; when?

12 ;?; where? where? me? me? ;?; ours?

13 petty petty lay lay Boyd Boyd Yale Yale

14 crux crux mix mix jinx jinx exits exits

15 today? today? Would you know? ;?;???

16 cucu cute cute scum scum cult cult cuff

17 chch chow chow ache ache ouch ouch much

18 bobo bowl bowl oboe oboe hobo hobo bone

19 DaDa Dave Dave Dawn Dawn Dale Dale Dane

PHRASE PRACTICE

(The diagonal bar which
separates the phrases
should not be typed.)

20 as you/you know/so that/for the/is that

21 you are/you may/we have/we know/that is

22 of this/on this/to you/to your/you will

23 for our/for your/from us/as the/as well

SPACING BETWEEN PARAGRAPHS

When single spacing is used (as it is here), leave a blank line between paragraphs. To do this, just return the carriage or carrier one extra time. In scoring timed writings, the extra blank line counts as 1 word.

SKILL CHECK

▷ Try to type 18 wam or
more for 2 minutes
within 4 errors.

24 The junior business club hosted a party   8

25 for the persons who live in the nursing   16

26 home.   17

27   18

28 Patients relaxed by the lake with quiet   26

29 games such as jigsaw puzzles, checkers,   34

30 and chess.   36

|1 |2 |3 |4 |5 |6 |7 |8

goal

Type 30 wam for 5 minutes within 4 errors.

TYPING TIP
☐ Use dashes instead of commas to set off nonessential elements that require special attention.

There is a typographical error in one of the paragraphs—the second one.

▷ **60-space line; single-space; tab 5; each line three times or more; double-space between *different* lines.**

WARMUP

1 Hal makes six dozen jugs of cider before every autumn game.

2 Here are the new percentages: 10%, 29%, 38%, 47%, and 56%.

3 Can you find the quote that needs to be placed on the page?

Edit as you type.

4 Put each topec on a seperate peice of paper for comparison.
|1 |2 |3 |4 |5 |6 |7 |8 |9 |10 |11 |12

PREVIEW

5 professional American everywhere attention October millions

6 acquires American competes organized April attracts cricket

7 season United States nearest popular baseball Red Stockings

SKILL CHECK

▷ **Remember to take at least two 1-minute timings before you check your 5-minute rate.**

8   When it's April in the United States, millions of fans   12

9 head for the nearest parks to play baseball or watch one of   24

10 the professional teams on opening day. Baseball is a sport   36

11 which grew out of a game called cricket. It is now popular   48

12 with folks everywhere. Professional baseball attracts most   60

13 of that attention, but almost all high schools and colleges   72

14 enjoy baseball.   75

15   The professional baseball teams are organized into the   87

16 American League and the National League. The first was the   99

17 National League. The Red Stockings, now known as the Reds,   111

18 made up the first team. The apex of the baseball season is   123

19 in October when the World Series is played. A team of each   135

20 league competes until one of them acquires four wins out of   147

21 seven games.   150
|1 |2 |3 |4 |5 |6 |7 |8 |9 |10 |11 |12 **SI: 1.43**

goals

Improve speed and accuracy with special drills. ☐ Use the tabulator key. ☐ Type 19 wam for 2 minutes within 4 errors.

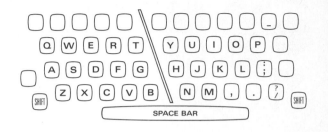

▷ **40-space line; single-space; each line three times or more; double-space between** *different* **lines.**

WARMUP

1 a;sldkfjghfjdksla;- a;sldkfjghfjdksla;/
2 mop ice axe gay cod nun sap wet Sam Vic
3 cozy wire quit gain boss lure avid Kate

AIM FOR ACCURACY

Try to type each word without pausing. Repeat the drill as often as necessary.

4 awe add aged crack area pave laity said
5 bee beg lab beat bout mobile board lobe
6 cat cab cage dance tack race cast peace
7 dew did dot added told debt divide odor
8 eat ear ever teeth east ream germ check

WORD PATTERNS

9 blbl blot blot able able ably ably blow
10 ovov over over cove cove rove rove move
11 elel else else pelt pelt reel reel sell
12 idid idle idle ride ride aide aide ibid
13 atat atom atom bath bath beat beat chat

PHRASE PRACTICE

14 we shall, we shall be glad, you will be
15 there is, there are, that are, they are
16 with our, with the, with them, with you
17 to know, to make, to me, to be, to take

60-2.
BOOK REPORT

▶ Type this draft of a book report, making corrections as noted. Refer to page 64 for revision marks.

6-inch line; single spacing.

Book Report, World Literature
Submitted to Mr. Anthony Leger
By Robin Leigh
January 10, 19--

THE ILIAD

The Author

    The _Iliad_ is a Greek epic traditionally attributed to a poet named Homer and dated about B.C. 850. Both the _Iliad_ and the _Odyssey_, also attributed to Homer, are based on the legend of the Trojan war and are the oldest surviving works of European literature.

The story

    The word _Iliad_ means the Tale of Ilios, that is, the Tale of Troy. Actually, Homer's theme is the Wrath of Achilles, a single event in the tenth year of the siege of troy. When Achilles was young, he was offered his choice of two lives: either he could remain in Greece and live to old age without glory, or he could go to Troy, win renown on the field of battle, and die young. Achilles chose to go to Troy. Both Agamemnon and Achilles fell in love with a Trojan girl named Briseis. When Agamemnon took Briseis away from the hero Achilles, ~~his prize of war, the captured girl Brieseis, Agamemnon~~ he robbed Achilles of the glory for which he had sacrificed the ease and long life he might have had in Greece. In great anger Achilles left the battlefield.

Without Achilles, the Greeks lost many battles. In an indirect way, then, Achilles ~~got his revenge.~~ was avenged.

Reaction

    The _Iliad_ is a fascinating story. ~~It is essentially a simple tale,~~ The plot was not as difficult to follow as I feared. ~~but the characters in it are very complex in the way they act out their roles.~~ The characters are noble, yet they also seem very human. I liked the poetry and am looking forward to reading the _Odyssey_.

18 able alto ajar airy apt air aid and ant
19 born bile boar body big bit boa bow box
20 clod coal clan char cut can cog cat cow
21 duty dice down dust dog dam did dot dug

22 ball hall fall dell yell cell sell jell
23 will hill mill sill lull mull null gull
24 lass mass pass bass loss toss boss moss
25 miss hiss kiss fuss muss cuss less mess
26 soot soon toot tool took wool wood woof

|1 |2 |3 |4 |5 |6 |7 |8

USING THE TABULATOR KEY

Your machine has a tabulator key or bar that can be used each time you want to indent. (Notice that the timing below indents the first line of the paragraph.) Follow these steps to use the tabulator:

1. Clear out any tabulator stops already set. Press the all-clear key if your machine has one, or move the carriage or carrier to the right margin. Hold down the tab-clear key as you return the carriage or carrier.

2. Set a tabulator stop where you wish the carriage to stop by moving the carriage or carrier to that point on the scale and pressing the set key.

3. Test the setting: return the carriage to the left margin and depress the tab bar or key (hold it down firmly until the carriage or carrier stops moving). It should stop where you set the tab stop.

Each time you use the tabulator in a timed writing, you are credited with one word (5 strokes).

Which tabular mechanisms are on your typewriter?

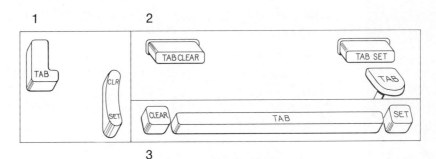

27 Dear Pat: 2

28   3

SKILL CHECK

D) Try to type this note
at 19 words a minute.
Single-space; after salu-
tation, double-space.

29   You said you wanted me to tell you   11
30 the time of the first track event. The   19
31 high jumps will begin at noon. This is   27
32 the first event I think you would enjoy   35
33 coming to see.   38

|1 |2 |3 |4 |5 |6 |7 |8

60

goals

Type minutes from handwritten copy. ☐
Type a report from corrected copy.

TYPING TIPS
☐ When you type from an edited draft, it is a good idea to read the draft before you begin to type, to make sure you understand the corrections.
☐ Titles of books should either be underscored or typed in all capitals. If you underscore, underscore spaces between words as well as the words themselves.

WARMUP

▶ Use lines 1–4 from Lesson 59 on page 112.

60-1. HANDWRITTEN MINUTES

▶ 6-inch line; single spacing; side headings.

SKILL CHECK

▶ Use the Skill Check from Lesson 59, p. 112.

Minutes of the Pep Club ^Meeting
March 27, 19— ^Representatives

Attendance
The second (meeting) ~~of the~~ monthly of the Trails High Pep Club representatives was held in the gymnasium at 3:30 p.m. Vice President Christi Spangenberg presided in the absence of the president.

Old Business
Marsha Kwo reported that the plans for "Spirit Week" are going well, and that signs may be posted on the walls if masking tape is used.
The plans for Black and Gold Day have also been approved according to Jay Steiner. On that day students will launch the sale of the black and gold T-shirts and scarves designed by Joanne Goldberg for the senior class fund.

New Business
June Metzer announced that the seniors are purchasing a new Elk mascot. It will be this year's senior gift to the school for the football team.
Mary Lyden ~~introduced~~ demonstrated a new cheer. The cheer was adopted for inclusion in the routine. It will be introduced at the ^April 6 basketball game.

Adjournment
The meeting adjourned at 4:30. The next meeting will be April 10.

Respectfully submitted,
Sydney Witherille, Secretary

12

goals

Improve speed and accuracy with special drills. ☐ Use shift lock key for all capitals. ☐ Type 20 wam for 2 minutes within 4 errors.

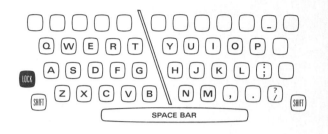

▶ **40-space line; single-space; each line three times or more; double-space between** *different* **lines.**

WARMUP

1 a;sldkfjgh,fjdksla; a;sldkfjgh.fjdksla;

2 ape bin coy ham his jaw box mob nor off

3 ever hawk just quad lazy pare raft rout

▶ **Try to type each word without pausing. Repeat the drill as often as necessary.**

AIM FOR ACCURACY

4 far fat deaf fuse after loaf fence fawn

5 get gas grab digit grant plug flag gear

6 him hum hope chalk sigh home ahead high

7 imp ill inject imply diet pain bite inn

8 jut joy major jammed reject joke jostle

▶ **Try to type each line four times in one minute. (32 words a minute!)**

BUILD SPEED

9 fig fit fix fib fir flat firm flag flap

10 fob fox for fur fun fame fish fine fair

11 gig got gus gut gob girl give gilt gown

12 hag hay ham hem hat heir hale half halt

|1 |2 |3 |4 |5 |6 |7 |8

TYPING ALL CAPITAL LETTERS

It's simple to type all capitals. Just follow these steps:

1. Press the shift lock. It is above one or both of the shift keys.

2. Type the words to be capitalized.

3. Release the shift lock by touching either shift key. *Be careful*—release the lock before typing a stroke that, like the hyphen, cannot be typed as a capital.

▶ **Each line three times or more; double-space between** *different* **lines.**

13 The name of the book is SCOTCH HEATHER.

14 Have you been to GA, ME, MN, TX, or WA?

▶ 6-inch line; single spacing; side headings. Shift 3 spaces to right for binding in club notebook. Triple-space before each side heading.

MINUTES OF THE GERMAN CLUB MEETING

January 28, 19--

ATTENDANCE

The regular monthly meeting of the South High German Club was held in Room C100 at 3:30 p.m., with all members present except Theresa Monk. Geoff Druffel presided at the meeting.

OLD BUSINESS

The Secretary read the minutes of the December meeting, and they were approved as read.

The Treasurer reported that there were two outstanding bills to be paid: $25.00 to Wells Grocery and $19.10 to South High Cafeteria. The balance on hand was $87.38.

NEW BUSINESS

Ingrid Ullery reported on plans for a trip to Hamburg in June. The travel agency can arrange for special rates for the group if reservations are made by February 15. Ingrid was asked by the President to acquire a list of those planning to go.

Arlen Coppock announced that the albums had arrived and would be distributed for sale immediately following the meeting.

ADJOURNMENT

The meeting adjourned at 4:15. The next meeting will be a special meeting held on February 14.

Respectfully submitted,

Martha Rivera, Secretary

15 oioi oily oily join join coin coin soil
16 shsh shag shag ashy ashy rash rash mash
17 rere read read area area pore pore bred
18 pipi pink pink spin spin epic epic pier
19 ieie died died lien lien lied lied lieu

BUILD SPEED

With practice on alter-
nate-hand letters

20 key jam irk icy fib if Irish idle giant
21 iris girl gland gist glad belt blame by
22 corn chap clan clap cue cow cub cur cud
23 did dig die dice down lamb lay cozy nap

▶ **Take three 30-second timings on each of these three very easy sentences.**

30-SECOND CHECK

Speed for ½ minute is
double the words typed.

24 Her new wigs did not fit her very well.
25 The very old cot in the attic was used.
26 A ball and bat can create a lot of fun.
  |1 |2 |3 |4 |5 |6 |7 |8

USING A SYLLABIC INTENSITY CODE

SI	Difficulty
1.00	Very Easy
1.15	Easy
1.25	Fairly Easy
1.35	Normal
1.45	Fairly Hard
1.55	Hard
1.65	Very Hard

Word Difficulty. The number of syllables contained in a word determines the difficulty of typing that word. An index called "Syllabic Intensity" averages out the number of syllables for all words in a piece of material. At the end of timed writings in this book you will see a notation like this: SI 1.04, referring to the Syllabic Intensity. The chart in the left margin will help you determine the difficulty of the material whenever the SI is indicated.

SKILL CHECK

▶ Set tab stop for 5-
space indentation. See if
you can type 20 or more
wam for 2 minutes
within 4 errors.

27 Dear Jill: 2
28   3
29   I urge you to see the county fair.   11
30 They even have a mini-type zoo for kids   19
31 of any age. I won a radio that runs on   27
32 a/c or d/c current. By the way, I know   35
33 a short cut--exit Quincy.   40
  |1 |2 |3 |4 |5 |6 |7 |8   SI: 1.18

59 goals

☐ Type 30 wam for 5 minutes within 4 errors.
☐ Type minutes in an attractive arrangement.

TYPING TIP
☐ Do not divide one-syllable words. Even when *ed* is added to some words, they still remain one-syllable words and cannot be divided.

weight   thought   scheme   shipped   passed

▶ **60-space line; single-space; each line three times or more; double-space between** *different* **lines.**

WARMUP

1 Jake quickly wove six scenes from the giant picture puzzle.

2 Our club made $10, $29, $38, $47, and $56 taking inventory.

3 You will be able to compose a report fast when you type it.

Edit as you type.

4 Develop a skil by faithful practise of your daily lessons.
|1 |2 |3 |4 |5 |6 |7 |8 |9 |10 |11 |12

PREVIEW

5 down jump ball game only stop both take from band last lead

6 feet skill floor crowd break every offense defense maneuver

7 buzzer quarter exercises fantastic continuous opportunities

SKILL CHECK

▶ **Typing 1-minute timings before taking the 5-minute checks will help you build your skill.**

8   Down on the floor, it's a continuous game of skill. A   12

9 jump ball begins the game, and only a referee's whistle can   24

10 stop it. It is a game where offense and defense count, for   36

11 preventing a basket is as important as making one. It is a   48

12 game that causes players to maneuver gracefully and to take   60

13 advantage of all opportunities. The team who does this the   72

14 best will win.   75

15   From the snappy warmup exercise with the brass band to   87

16 that last resounding buzzer of the final quarter of play, a   99

17 game of basketball brings excitement. Sitting in a special   111

18 section for cheering and following the cheerleaders as they   123

19 lead the crowd in support of the team is great fun. Seeing   135

20 a fantastic steal or fast break will bring the crowd to its   147

21 feet to cheer.   150
|1 |2 |3 |4 |5 |6 |7 |8 |9 |10 |11 |12 **SI: 1.43**

goals

Improve performance on all keys from Lessons 1–8 using intensive, special drills. ☐ Type 20 wam for 2 minutes within 4 errors.

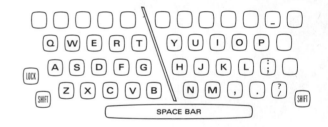

UPWARD REACHES

▶ 40-space line; single-space; each line three times or more; double-space between *different* lines.

TWO CLINIC ROUTINES

20-Minute Activity

Skill Check: 1 copy

Drills: odd-numbered lines once; even-numbered lines twice

Skill Check: 2 tries or until goal is reached

40-Minute Activity

Skill Check: 3 copies

Drills: odd-numbered lines, twice; even-numbered lines three times

Skill Check: 4 tries or until goal is achieved

1 sit yes low kit dew word wish soar door
2 lot dot rid pat sup foul sore wide tilt
3 hop top par pan rid year pile kept spin
4 rate under lower aqua jolt result yield

5 six cat van can car vamp lamb sack save
6 bid ban nab sob nag vane box waxen, ace
7 mid map mad ham man mace name calm acme
8 Zed Bud zebra razz cram exact came Anne

9 desk skill glad glade shall lash as sag
10 shake gall laff ladle shall dash saddle
11 led lag ads ale all less cash dash gash
12 ash led oak gag hag dark deal flag shag

13 tick dove pals firm code josh form open
14 pane pale town rove aide bent bode born
15 convoy key slang proxy bible chap blame
16 elbow ensue fight audit lapel high iron

SKILL CHECK

▶ Try to type 20 wam or more for 2 minutes with 4 or fewer errors. Single-space; after salutation and between paragraphs, double-space.

17 Dear Jackie: 3
18   4
19 The winter ice-carving events will open   12
20 with a gala party at Breeze Field. Due   20
21 to the extra space set aside this year,   28
22 a larger quantity of ice will be given.   36
23   37
24 Will you come?   40

|1 |2 |3 |4 |5 |6 |7 |8   SI: 1.22

58

goal

Format and compose a simple news release.

WARMUP

▶ **Use lines 1–4 from Lesson 57 on page 109.**

58-1.
NEWS RELEASE

▶ **6-inch line; double spacing. Type the heading block as shown.**

58-2.
▶ **Try to compose a news release on your own. Suppose that your school's debate team just won first in the state. How would you write the release?**

SKILL CHECK

▶ **Use the Skill Check from Lesson 57, p. 109.**

CENTRAL HIGH SCHOOL

N E W S   R E L E A S E   Mallard, Iowa 50563

Release: Immediately

From: David Rompani, Principal

BAND AND CHEERLEADERS TO MARCH AT PEACH BOWL
↓3

Mallard, Iowa, November 20—Central High School Band and Cheerleaders have just received word that they will receive an invitation to march in this year's Peach Bowl Parade in Atlanta. The local high school groups were chosen from over 2000 marching units throughout the nation.

Mr. Gerald Markworth, band director, remarked: "This is a great opportunity for these young people. They have been waiting with great hope that they would be among those selected, and have been working hard to be ready for the event. They are in great form."

The Cheerleaders have won seven national championships with their precision drills, but this is the first time they have succeeded in their goal to perform in a Bowl game. Mrs. Roberta Crum, sponsor, says that they have developed a new routine to perform with the band for the halftime show.

Plans for a charter flight to Atlanta on Friday, December 8, are being finalized. Any students and parents who would like to accompany the groups should contact Mr. Markworth by November 30.

goals

Control 1, 2, and 3 keys. □ Type 20 or more wam for 2 minutes within 4 errors. □ Center words horizontally.

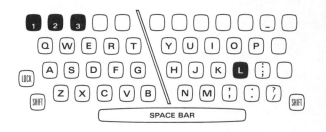

▶ **40-space line; single-space; each line three times or more; double-space between *different* lines.**

WARMUP

1 ab—cd—ef—gh—ij—kl—mn—op—qr—st—uv—wx—yz—

2 Jack was vexed by a long quip from Zoe.

3 Sue may go to the mall for a blue coat.

1 KEY

Use A finger. (Note: If your machine does not have a number 1 key, use the small letter l.)

4 aqa aq1 a1a 111 a1a 111 a1a 1:11, 1,111

5 1.1, 11 ads, 11 ants, 11 acts, 11 axles

6 My 11 aides typed 11 ads in 11 minutes.

2 KEY

Use S finger.

7 sws sw2 s2s 222 s2s 222 s2s 2:22, 2,222

8 2.2, 22 sets, 22 seas, 22 sums, 22 sips

9 The 12 girls won 21 games of 22 played.

3 KEY

Use D finger.

10 ded de3 d3d 333 d3d 333 d3d 3:33, 3,333

11 3.3, 33 dips, 33 dens, 33 dots, 33 dues

12 The 23 girls found 323 bags in 13 days.

NEW KEY REINFORCEMENT

13 Anna typed pages 11, 12, and 13 for me.

14 Make 12 copies of pages 23—31 by 11:22.

15 Flight 312 will land at 2:31 on Friday.

SKILL CHECK

▶ Try to type this note once in 2 minutes within 4 errors. If you can, you are typing 20 words a minute.

16 Vic kicked 21 yards before the first 13   8

17 minutes had gone by. Rex was almost 12   16

18 yards from a goal, but he could not zip   24

19 the ball quickly to score the points on   32

20 the board. The home team jumped ahead.   40

|1 |2 |3 |4 |5 |6 |7 |8   SI: 1.10

FORMATTING A ONE-PAGE REPORT

By (Your Name) ↓3

When one is formatting a one-page report, it is important that the content be concise and that the report look attractive and be easy to read. Here are some suggestions which will be helpful.

First, if you are typing a final copy, begin the title on line 13. Drop down two lines and center "By" and your name under the title. Drop down three lines to begin the first paragraph. If you are typing a draft, plan the placement according to the exact length of the report. After you have edited the report, count the number of lines the report will take and plan the placement so the report is centered vertically on the page.

Second, the line length is usually 60 spaces--30 spaces on each side of the center. If the report is to be bound at the left, however, move the entire line of writing over three spaces to the right.

Third, the bottom margin should be one and one-half to two inches deep. A balance line can be added if the margin is too deep.

Fourth, double-space the report so that it will be easy to read. If the report will not fit on one page, and cannot be cut, it is acceptable to single-space it.

Balance Line——— January 4, 19--

▶ Read the report completely before you type it.

Copy the report exactly as it appears if you use pica spacing, but allow for different line endings if you are using elite spacing.

You will also have more spaces between your last line and the balance line if you use elite spacing.

OPERATING THE BACKSPACER

▷ Use a half sheet of paper for the following exercise.

Find the backspace key at the top left or right of the keyboard. Practice using it. Now line up three words at the center. First, set a tab stop at the center (50). For each word, tab to the center, then backspace once for each letter in the word. Type the word.

```
          Team
        Captain
        Schedule
```

CENTERING HORIZONTALLY

▷ Use a half sheet of paper for the following exercise.

1. Set the carriage or carrier at the center (50). Set a tab stop.
2. Say the strokes (including spaces) to yourself in pairs. Depress the backspace key once after each pair. Don't backspace for an odd letter left over.
3. Type the material. It should be in the middle of your paper.

```
WINTER OLYMPIC SPORTS
        skiing
        skating
        swimming
```

CENTERING TASKS

▷ 13–1 to 13–4. Use a half sheet of paper for each task. Double-space; center each line. Start: 13–1 on line 12; 13–2 on line 11; 13–3 on line 10; 13–4 on line 9.

13-1

```
parachuting
mountain climbing
spelunking
tobogganing
snowmobiling
```

13-2

```
lacrosse
table tennis
jai alai
handball
golf
rugby
```

13-3

surfing
fishing
sailing
canoeing
scuba diving
yachting
racing

13-4

fencing
football
boxing
hunting
kayaking
dancing
exercising
skiing

goals

Type 30 wam for 5 minutes with 4 errors or less. ☐ Format a simple one-page report.

TYPING TIP
☐ EI and IE Words

Put *i* before *e* except after *c*, or when sounded like *a* as in *neighbor* and *weigh*.

▶ **60-space line; single-space; each line three times or more; double-space between** *different* **lines.**

WARMUP

1 Put the index form jobs in alphabetical order very quickly.

2 Please take jobs 10, 29, 38, 47, and 56 to zones 29 and 14.

3 It is easy to type a report if you have the skill to do so.

Edit as you type.

4 Have you recieved my report about writting business leters?

|1 |2 |3 |4 |5 |6 |7 |8 |9 |10 |11 |12

PREVIEW

▶ **Practice these words from the timing below.**

5 wrap furry school cheering football clapping different view

6 execute exact mixture accident successful professional zeal

SKILL CHECK

▶ **Try to type 30 words a minute for 5 minutes.**

Take a 1-minute timing on each paragraph before checking your skill for 5 minutes.

7   Wrap up in a big blanket, cover your head with a furry   12

8 hat, and warm your hands by clapping to cheer your favorite   24

9 football team to victory. Football is a popular sport, and   36

10 it draws millions to stadiums to view high school, college,   48

11 and professional players tackle, block, punt, and score. A   60

12 faithful pigskin fan will endure rain and snow to watch one   72

13 final big play.   75

14   The antics on the field are quite a bit different from   87

15 the cheering in the stands. It takes a mixture of zeal and   99

16 talent to make a football team successful. Each player has   111

17 spent many hours learning and practicing just to execute at   123

18 the exact moment. It's not very often that a pass or block   135

19 can be made by sheer accident, or that a touchdown does not   147

20 bring a smile.   150

|1 |2 |3 |4 |5 |6 |7 |8 |9 |10 |11 |12   **SI: 1.36**

goals

Control 4, 5, and 6 keys.
□ Type 20 or more wam
for 2 minutes within 4
errors. □ Block center
words.

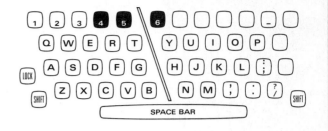

▶ **40-space line; single-space; each line three times or more; double-space between *different* lines.**

WARMUP

1 Joseph zipped around the track quickly.
2 Ed made 23 hats in 13 days for 12 guys.
3 It is nice to smile when you can do it.

4 KEY

Use F finger.

4 frf fr4 f4f 444 f4f 444 f4f 4:44, 4,444
5 4.4, 44 fats, 44 fits, 44 fins, 44 fads
6 I saw 44 floats at the fairs on July 4.

5 KEY

Use F finger.

7 frf fr5 f5f 555 f5f 555 f5f 5:55, 5,555
8 5.5, 55 fans, 55 foes, 55 figs, 55 fell
9 Roger will be 15 on the 25th of August.

6 KEY

Use J finger.

10 jyj jy6 j6j 666 j6j 666 j6j 6:66, 6,666
11 6.6, 66 jabs, 66 jets, 66 jugs, 66 jobs
12 Can 65 boys make 546 cakes by April 26?

NEW KEY REINFORCEMENT

13 Katie ran 2 laps in 4 minutes at 12:33.
14 To win, he typed 56 words in 5 minutes.
15 Marlis came in 3, 4, or 5 in the match.
16 Route 312 is farther than is Route 465.

SKILL CHECK

▶ If you can type this note in 2 minutes within 4 errors, you're typing 20 words a minute.

17 The sale of 462 antiques to Zeke amazed   8
18 us. Joven said 35 percent of the goods   16
19 sold by 12 a.m., and the rest by 5 p.m.   24
20 Can Max work Friday? I will need quite   32
21 a big crew to manage the 564 paintings.   40

|1 |2 |3 |4 |5 |6 |7 |8   SI: 1.17

56-1. TABLE OF CONTENTS

▶ 5-inch line, tabs at 4, center, and right margin. Center vertically. Number the contents page "ii" and center the number one inch from bottom of page. Do not consider "ii" in vertical centering.

The contents page is really an outline.

T A B L E   O F   C O N T E N T S ↓3

tab

Flashback Into the History of Business Education ↓2		1
	1. Historical Development of Accounting	1
	2. Historical Development of Distributive Education	9
	3. Historical Development of Office Education	19
Key Issues Which Challenge Business Educators		25
	1. Cooperative Vocational Education	25
	2. Consumer Education	38
	3. Teaching Typewriting	51
Gazing Into the Future of Business Education		70
	1. Economic Literacy	70
	2. Education for Employment	75
BIBLIOGRAPHY		80

56-2. TABLE OF CONTENTS WITH LEADERS

▶ 4-inch line, tabs at 4, center, and right margin. Center vertically.

Leaders (a row of periods) may be used to lead from title to page numbers. A row of periods must begin and end with at least one space.

CONTENTS

I.	Purpose	1
II.	Research	1
	A. Sources	1
	B. Procedures	2
III.	Findings	3
	A. Multi-Channel Equipment	3
	B. Playback Devices	5
	C. Monitoring Methods	6
IV.	Summary	8
	Bibliography	10

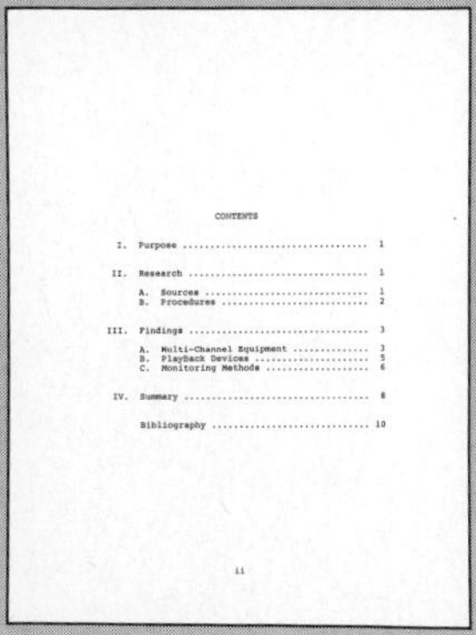

▶ **Use a half sheet of paper for the following exercise.**

Many times you will need to backspace before setting the left margin. Use the following drill to practice doing this. Backspace the first line of this drill; then set the left margin stop. The three lines will then line up.

HOW TO PLAY TENNIS

Illustrated by

Janet Dillon

BLOCK CENTERING

Block centering means to center a *block* of lines rather than individual lines. To block-center, follow this procedure after making sure that the margin stops are out of the way:

1. Pick the longest line in the group.
2. Backspace to center that line.
3. Set the left margin stop.
4. Begin all the lines at the margin stop.

▶ **Now try this practice drill. Use a half sheet of paper and block-center the following lines.**

When you block-center,
all the lines are even
at the left margin.

BLOCK-CENTERING TASKS

▶ **14-1 to 14-4. Use a half sheet of paper for each task. Double-space; begin on line 10; leave 2 spaces after the period following a number; and block-center the list.**

14-1
1. archery
2. backpacking
3. bobsledding
4. basketball
5. baseball
6. badminton

14-2
1. canoeing
2. camping
3. croquet
4. chess
5. cycling
6. exploring

14-3
1. squash
2. volleyball
3. wrestling
4. walking
5. weight lifting
6. yachting

14-4
1. fishing
2. snow sculpturing
3. reading
4. parachuting
5. horseback riding
6. ballooning

56

goals

To type 29 wam on a 5-minute timing. □ Type a table of contents. □ Type leaders.

WARMUP

1   The Weather Watchers' organization met after the huge snow.

2   Animals are such agreeable friends: they cannot criticize.

3   Harold owes me $1.10 but wants to settle for 80¢, or 72.7%.

Edit as you type.

4   please introduce professor otto and my father to the group.
|1 |2 |3 |4 |5 |6 |7 |8 |9 |10 |11 |12

AIM FOR ACCURACY

Practice shifting technique.

5   Frank Louis Candy Mitch Stan Myra Walt Joey Dan Kim Ray Ike

6   Doris Marty Queen Jason Dora Jack Bill Paul Alf Kay Pam Tom

7   Frank told Milt that Carl and Paul dated Dot and Pam White.

SKILL CHECK

▶ Try to type 29 words a minute on a 5-minute timing within 4 errors.

8   Many sports require a lot of time in physical exercise   12

9   to get in trim for the game, and certainly wrestling is not   24

10 to be excluded from this situation. Muscles, joints, back,   36

11 arms, legs must be conditioned over a period of time before   48

12 being put to the test in a wrestling match with an opponent   60

13 who will try to pin the competitor's shoulder to the floor.   72

14 This causes wrestling to be one of the toughest sports, and   84

15 one that also demands a high degree of skill and knowledge.   96

16 Thousands of wrestlers in high school and college take part   108

17 in amateur matches that are divided according to categories   120

18 of weight. In total there are eight weight sizes. Persons   132

19 are assigned to a division and may not compete outside that   144

20 class.   145

|1 |2 |3 |4 |5 |6 |7 |8 |9 |10 |11 |12 **SI: 1.44**

goals

Control 7, 8, and 9 keys.
☐ Type 20 or more wam for 2 minutes within 4 errors. ☐ Center groups of words vertically and horizontally on a page.

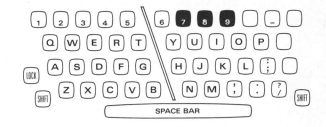

▶ 40-space line; single-space; each line three times or more; double-space between *different* lines.

WARMUP

1 Liz gave her extra blue quilt to Cindy.
2 I sang in 34 shows, over 21 or 22 days.
3 If he can see it today, he may keep it.

7 KEY
Use J finger.

4 juj ju7 j7j 777 j7j 777 j7j 7:77, 7,777
5 7.7, 77 joys, 77 jots, 77 jets, 77 juts
6 Larry was 17 in the contest of 77 boys.

8 KEY
Use K finger.

7 kik ki8 k8k 888 k8k 888 k8k 8:88, 8,888
8 8.8, 88 kits, 88 keys, 88 kegs, 88 kids
9 Linda arrived at 8 p.m. with 178 songs.

9 KEY
Use L finger.

10 1o1 1o9 191 999 191 999 191 9:99, 9,999
11 9.9, 99 logs, 99 legs, 99 lots, 99 laws
12 Do you know that 79 men sailed in 1789?

NEW KEY REINFORCEMENT

13 He plans to be here May 17, 18, and 19.
14 Sally has won 98 trophies in 179 tries.
15 Can she type 19 letters in 178 minutes?
16 Jake will buy 796 chairs and 98 tables.

SKILL CHECK

▶ Try to type 20 or more wam for 2 minutes within 4 errors.

17 Vi: The 12 bike trails near your house   8
18 are quite strenuous. Can we ride on 3,   16
19 6, and 8 the next time? Will you check   24
20 4, 5, 7, and 9, too? Let me say thanks   32
21 again; I am enjoying the exercise. Liz   40

|1 |2 |3 |4 |5 |6 |7 |8   SI: 1.19

Three styles of cover pages are shown. In each case, the information on the title is positioned in the upper half (33 spaces in each half), and the remaining information is positioned in the lower half. In the spread-center and center styles, each line is centered. In the pivot style, all lines end evenly at the right margin.

To pivot lines so they end at the right margin: (1) move the carriage or carrier 1 space beyond the point where you want a line to end; (2) backspace once for every letter and space in the line; (3) type the line.

The cover page is numbered "i," but the "i" is not typed on the page.

▶ **55-1. Type each of the three styles of cover (title) pages illustrated below; use full sheet for each one.**

▶ **55-2. You have just completed your term paper on Methods to Conserve Energy. It is due today for your class in Consumer Education. Mr. Carl Amado is the instructor. Design a cover page for your report. Prepare a rough draft copy of your cover page, and then retype to make a professional-looking copy.**

▶ **55-3. Select a different design for your cover page and type it using the information from 55-2.**

A. Spread-Center

B. Center

C. Pivot

```
S P E C I A L   R E P O R T

O N

THE ROLE OF WOMEN IN THE WORK FORCE



Prepared for

Mrs. JoEllen Green

by

Harry Marks

January 15, 19--
```

```
SPECIAL REPORT ON

THE ROLE OF WOMEN IN THE WORK FORCE

by Harry Marks




American History
Mrs. JoEllen Green
Northern University

January 15, 19--
```

```
SPECIAL REPORT ON

THE ROLE OF WOMEN IN THE WORK FORCE
_____

By Harry Marks




Prepared for
American History
Mrs. JoEllen Green
January 15, 19--
```

COUNTING VERTICAL LINES

Before you learn how to center typed copy vertically on a page, you need to know about the vertical line count of a sheet of 8½″ × 11″ paper.

▷ Insert a half sheet of paper and type the word *single* six times; then measure the lines with a ruler to see how much space they occupy.

Most typewriters space 6 vertical lines to an inch. Standard typing paper is 11 inches long, so you can get 11 × 6 = 66 lines on a full page or 33 lines on a half page. Some special and imported typewriters space 5¼ lines to an inch, giving 57 lines on a full page and 28 lines on a half page. "A4" metric paper is slightly longer—70 lines to the page.

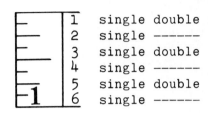

1	single double
2	single -------
3	single double
4	single -------
5	single double
6	single -------

CENTERING VERTICALLY

For material to look centered vertically, the top margin must be a line or two narrower than the bottom margin. To center a group of lines and provide this desirable difference:

1. Count the lines (including blank ones) that the material will occupy.
2. Subtract that number from the number of lines you can type on the paper.

3. Divide the difference by 2 (count a fraction as a whole number) to find the number of the line, counting from the top, on which you should begin.

Example: To center 7 double-spaced lines on a half sheet, you need 13 lines (7 typed, 6 blank); 33 − 13 = 20, and 20 ÷ 2 = 10, the line on which to begin typing.

CENTERING TASKS

▷ Use a half sheet of paper for each task.

15-1. Center vertically; double-space; leave 1 space before and after the hyphen for this special display; center each line horizontally.

15-2. Center vertically; double-space; leave 1 space before and after the hyphen for this special display; block-center horizontally.

When you have finished, fold the paper top to bottom and crease it at the center. The same number of characters should be to the left and the right of the crease.

15-1

ANNUAL DOG SHOW

Monday Evening, May 16, 19—

6:45 – Poodle and Schnauzer

7:45 – Pekingese and Pomeranian

8:45 – Dalmatian and Lhasa Apso

9:45 – Maltese and Pug

Tuesday Morning, May 17, 19—

10:00 – Presentation of Awards

15-2

ANNUAL DOG SHOW

Monday Evening, May 16, 19—

6:45 – Poodle and Schnauzer

7:45 – Pekingese and Pomeranian

8:45 – Dalmatian and Lhasa Apso

9:45 – Maltese and Pug

Tuesday Morning, May 17, 19—

10:00 – Presentation of Awards

goals

Type 29 wam on a 5-minute timing. □ Type several variations of a cover (title) page.

WARMUP

1　Your paper was quoted extensively at the junior league tea.

2　Year after year, nature paints pictures of infinite beauty.

3　Two hyphens make up a dash--leave no space before or after.

Edit as you type.

4　can you take another trip to the south this fall or winter?
　　|1　|2　|3　|4　|5　|6　|7　|8　|9　|10　|11　|12

BIBLIOGRAPHY

▶ **Type this in correct form; use full sheet.**

Ordinal numbers may be abbreviated this way—

first	1st
second	2d
third	3d
fourth	4th

Balsley, I. W., Dictation Tests, National Collegiate Association of Secretaries, Texas Tech University, Lubbock, TX, 1973.

Buros, O. K. (ed.), The Sixth Mental Measurements Yearbook, Gryphone Press, Highland Park, NJ, 1965.

Kennedy, J. J., The Use and Misuse of Analysis of Covariance," NABTE Review, 1977, pp. 10-11.

SKILL CHECK

▶ **Try to type 29 words a minute on a 5-minute timing with 4 or fewer errors.**

5　　　If you have used dumbbells and barbells, you know of a　12

6　unique sport: the sport of weight lifting. It is featured　24

7　in competition between and among those who have developed a　36

8　truly great strength with their muscles. Competition takes　48

9　place according to weight divisions that are just about the　60

10　same as those used for boxing. The muscle development that　72

11　is obtained by lifting weights is also used by athletes for　84

12　maximizing their body tone to compete in other sports.　95

13　　　You may see three types of lifts in the weight lifting　107

14　events. One is the military press whereby the person lifts　119

15　the barbell off the floor, then rests it against the chest;　131

16　a second type is the clean and press; the third is known as　143

17　the snatch.　145
　　|1　|2　|3　|4　|5　|6　|7　|8　|9　|10　|11　|12　**SI:** 1.37

16

goals

Control 0, ½, and ¼ keys. □ Type 20 wam for 2 minutes within 4 errors. □ Center announcements vertically and horizontally. □ Spread letters.

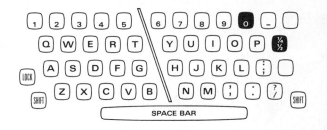

> **D** 40-space line; single-space; each line three times or more; double-space between *different* lines.

WARMUP

1 Bix moved quickly from popular to jazz.

2 The winners were: 29, 38, 47, and 156.

3 Mandy will go to the game when she can.

0 KEY

Use Sem finger.

4 ;p; ;p0 ;0; 000 ;0; 000 ;0; 1:00, 1,000

5 1.00, 100 parts, 100 plants, 100 plates

6 He left at 10:00 a.m. with 1,000 pumps.

½ KEY

Use Sem finger.

7 ;p; ;p½ ;½; ½½½ ;½; ½½½ ;½; ½½½ ;½; ½½½

8 10½, 29½, 38½, 47½, 56½, 38 1/2, 49 1/2

9 Linda has ½ of it; who has the other ½?

¼ ½ KEY

Use Sem finger.

10 ;p; ;p¼ ;¼; ¼¼¼ ;¼; ¼¼¼ ;¼; ¼¼¼ ;¼; ¼¼¼

11 10¼, 29¼, 38¼, 47¼, 56¼, 29 1/4, 56 1/4

12 Can ¼ of them give ¼ of their time now?

NEW KEY REINFORCEMENT

13 Don worked 5½ hours; Sally worked 103¼.

14 Add 786 1/4 and 39 1/4 to make 825 1/2.

15 Ursula sold 385½ pies, Kathy sold 649¼.

16 Yes, I can give ¼, but I cannot give ½.

SKILL CHECK

> **D** Try to type this note once in 2 minutes within 4 errors. If you can, you are typing 20 words a minute.

17 Dear Jake: State tennis matches at the   8

18 Baxone College courts have been set for   16

19 August 27, 28, and 29. We will present   24

20 entries from all the 164 schools in our   32

21 Region 350. Can you come? Quint Zabar   40

|1 |2 |3 |4 |5 |6 |7 |8   SI: 1.24

54-1. BIBLIOGRAPHY

▶ 5-inch line; tabs at 10 and center; center on page.

Two authors

Same author

Organization as author

tab

Bloom, B. S., <u>Human Characteristics and School Learning</u>, McGraw–Hill Book Company, New York, 1976. ↓2

Carroll, John, and Peter Davies, <u>The American Heritage Word Frequency Book</u>, Houghton Mifflin Company, Boston, 1972.

Thorndike, Richard L., "Reading as Reasoning," <u>Reading Research Quarterly</u>, Winter, 1973–74, pp. 135–147.

------, <u>Reading Comprehension Education in Fifteen Countries</u>, John Wiley & Sons, New York, 1973.

U.S. Bureau of the Census, <u>Eighteenth Census of the United States, 1960</u>, Government Printing Office, Washington, 1961.

SKILL CHECK

▶ Try to type 29 words a minute on a 5-minute timing with 4 or fewer errors.

5	Tennis anyone? I am sure you have heard that question	12
6	many times in just the past few months. This sport engages	24
7	the interest of many. Tennis is good exercise. Persons of	36
8	any age can learn to use the racquet. Tennis can trace its	48
9	roots back to ancient Greece and the game of handball. The	60
10	early French gazettes reported news on a game quite similar	72
11	to present tennis matches.	77
12	Though tennis is most often played outdoors, there has	89
13	been in recent years a great growth of indoor facilities to	101
14	permit year–round play. Two or four people may play in one	113
15	game. Points are given by hitting a ball so that the rival	125
16	is not able to return it over the net and inside the court.	137
17	The first match was held at Wimbledon.	145

|1 |2 |3 |4 |5 |6 |7 |8 |9 |10 |11 |12   **SI: 1.37**

54-2. ENUMERATION

▶ Center longest line; tabs at 4 and center; single spacing but double-space between numerical listings.

Type the information presented on the previous page in "To Type a Bibliography." Display it on a full sheet of paper. Type a rough draft; then retype, centering vertically and horizontally.

SPREADING LETTERS

When you want to make words and/or headings look special, spread them out by leaving 1 space between letters and 3 spaces between words. Here is an example:

Y e s ,   I   c a n .

▶ **To help visualize the spacing between letters and words, try this exercise. Type 33 hyphens and under them spread:** Ready, play ball.

R e a d y ,   p l a y   b a l l .

▶ **Now type 45 hyphens and under them spread:** My, Oh, My, What a Day.

CENTERING TASKS

▶ **16-1. Half sheet; double-space; center each line as shown.**

▶ **16-2. Full sheet; double-space; spread-center the first line; center other lines.**

▶ **16-3. Full sheet; double-space; center each line as shown.**

▶ **16-4. Half sheet; double-space; spread-center the first line; center other lines.**

16-1

A T T E N T I O N

ALL CHESS PLAYERS

Come to Room 284C

at 3:30 p.m.

Monday, September 15

J O I N   T H E   F U N

16-2

NOTICE
The Snow Flake Club
will hold its
MONTHLY MEETING
November 1, 19--
at 8:00 p.m.

16-3

THE POETRY CLUB

cordially invites you

for dinner

at 6:00 p.m.

Wednesday, October 3, 19--

16-4

FOR SALE
1977 Chevy Van
Custom-Designed Interior
CB Radio and Antenna
Excellent Condition
Call 349-8257

53-2. OUTLINE

▶ **Center longest line plus one roman numeral; tabs at 4, 8, and center; single spacing; center vertically on page.**

To type "I" outside the margin, press both margin release and backspace.

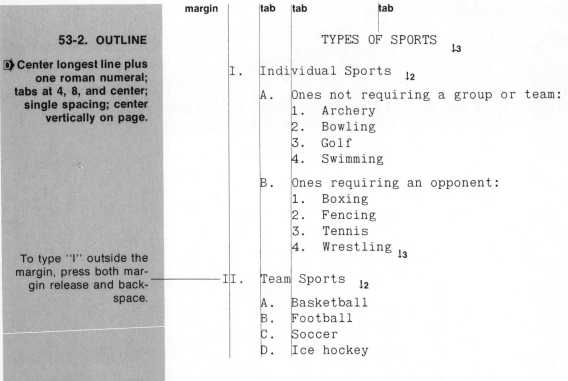

```
        margin    tab   tab        tab

                      TYPES  OF  SPORTS  ↓3

             I.   Individual Sports  ↓2

                  A.   Ones not requiring a group or team:
                       1.   Archery
                       2.   Bowling
                       3.   Golf
                       4.   Swimming

                  B.   Ones requiring an opponent:
                       1.   Boxing
                       2.   Fencing
                       3.   Tennis
                       4.   Wrestling  ↓3

             II.  Team Sports  ↓2

                  A.   Basketball
                  B.   Football
                  C.   Soccer
                  D.   Ice hockey
```

54

goals

Type 29 wam on a 5-minute timing. □ Type a bibliography.

> **TYPING TIP**
> □ Capitalize every *proper noun,* that is, the official name of a particular person, place, or thing.
>
> | | |
> |---|---|
> | James E. Carter | Friday, July 7 |
> | Boise, Idaho | the New Deal |
> | Ford Motor Company | the Chinese |
> | the United Fund | Venus and Mercury |

WARMUP

1 Grab the reverse lever if it varies a degree off precision.

2 Ignore ones who will want to challenge your ability to win.

3 It took 246 7/8 pounds to fill the 4 x 6 storage bin there.

Edit as you type.

4 i took history 401, english 411, and physics 302 this term.

```
|1   |2   |3   |4   |5   |6   |7   |8   |9   |10  |11  |12
```

TO TYPE A BIBLIOGRAPHY

1. Begin each item with the author's name; type the last name first.
   a. If there is more than one author, invert the first author's name only.
   b. When an organization is listed as the author, do not invert the name.
2. Arrange items in alphabetic sequence.

3. Indent the run-over lines 10 spaces.
4. Underscore the name of a book or magazine.
5. Use quotation marks around the title of a magazine article or chapter in a book.
6. When there are several works by the same author, replace the author's name after its first use with a dash made of 6 hyphens, or a rule made of 10 underscores. Then list the works alphabetically by title.

goals

Build skill with special drills. □ Type 22 wam for 2 minutes within 4 errors. □ Center a handwritten message on a full sheet.

▶ **40-space line; single-space; tabs at 5 and center; each line three times or more; double-space between *different* lines.**

WARMUP

1 It takes zip to excite the large crowd.
2 August 2, 1738, was when 564 were seen.
3 Quite a few men and boys are very just.
  |1 |2 |3 |4 |5 |6 |7 |8

30-SECOND CHECK

▶ Do the 30-second check twice; then do it twice again after you practice lines 7–12.

4 How many games will they play by today?
5 She is happy when he can win the match.
6 It is fun to go hiking in the warm sun.
  |1 |2 |3 |4 |5 |6 |7 |8

BUILD SPEED

With practice on double letters

7 seem pool miss tool eggs door ebbs ooze
8 ditto hilly class skill essay annoy zoo
9 fiddle puppet dizzy bullet robber rummy

AIM FOR ACCURACY

With practice on one-hand words

10 edge pink dead link debt inky face mink
11 west polo axes look text oily fast milk
12 daze limp acre pump data pill wave only

SKILL CHECK

▶ Try to type this note in 2 minutes within 4 errors.

13 Dear Zigg: 2
14   3
15   We are planning a hike for one day   11
16 early in the fall. Quite a few members 19
17 have taken the trip before and say that 27
18 it is well worth our time. Please come 35
19 and join us for some fun.   40
20   41
21   Dixie   44
  |1 |2 |3 |4 |5 |6 |7 |8   SI: 1.12

goals

Type 28 wam on a 5-minute timing. ☐ Type an enumeration within an outline.

WARMUP

1 It remains a puzzle how anyone could jar the exit sign off.

2 Seldom does nature say one thing and wisdom something else.

3 Oranges are selling @ 40¢ a pound and lettuce @ 49¢ a head.

Insert vowels.

4 —ntern—tion—l tr—ck ev—nts ar— c—mm—nly me—sur—d —n m—ters.
|1 |2 |3 |4 |5 |6 |7 |8 |9 |10 |11 |12

SKILL CHECK

▶ Try to type 28 words a minute on a 5-minute timing with 4 or fewer errors.

5 Did you ever glide a sled without runners? If so, you were   12

6 having fun at tobogganing! Tobogganing is the winter sport   24

7 of coasting on snow or ice with a runnerless sled. Usually   36

8 four people make up a team; the one at the rear does all of   48

9 the steering. A very great speed is achieved on the slopes   60

10 of snow-capped peaks with this brand of sled. Hunters from   72

11 diverse Indian tribes built toboggans to track game quickly   84

12 over the snows. Indians had to make their sleds from bark.   96

13 Eskimos at this time used whalebone for sleds. But you may   108

14 enjoy the excitement of a fast, great, crazy ride——so try a   120

15 bobsled. Bobsledding is an offshoot of tobogganing. Rides   132

16 can peak at speeds of 90 miles an hour.   140
|1 |2 |3 |4 |5 |6 |7 |8 |9 |10 |11 |12 SI: 1.37

**53-1.
ENUMERATION**

▶ 5-inch line; single spacing; center vertically on page.

HOW TO TYPE AN OUTLINE

1. Determine the left margin set by centering the longest line, including the first roman numeral.

2. Indent each step four spaces. Each key letter or number should be followed by a period and 2 spaces.

3. Leave 2 blank lines before and 1 blank line after a line that begins with a roman numeral.

17-1

17-2

▷ 17-1. Center verti- cally on half sheet; spread-center the first line and center other lines horizontally. Triple-space after first line; double-space the rest.

▷ 17-2. Center verti- cally and block-center horizontally on half sheet. Triple-space after first line; double-space the rest.

WELCOME PARTY
Sponsored by the French Club
TO HONOR EXCHANGE STUDENTS
Saturday, January 26, 19--
at 6:00 p.m.
Olympia Recreation Center
4853 Wellington Street

What: W E L C O M E   P A R T Y

Who: Sponsored by the French Club

Why: TO HONOR EXCHANGE STUDENTS

When: Saturday, January 26, 19--

at 6:00 p.m.

Where: Olympia Recreation Center

4853 Wellington Street

goals

Build skill with special drills.   □ Type 22 wam for 2 minutes within 4 errors.   □ Learn variations of centering on a full sheet.

TYPING TIPS
□ Do not space after a colon when it is used to denote time (6:15).
□ Do space before and after a hyphen when it is used to separate differing items (6:15 – Dentist).

▷ 40-space line; single-space; tabs at 5 and center; each line three times or more; double-space between *different* lines.

WARMUP

1 My boys saw six quiet lions at the zoo.
2 I can type 10, 29, 38, 47, and 56 well.
3 Did they jump very far at Greg's track?

|1 |2 |3 |4 |5 |6 |7 |8

30-SECOND CHECK

▷ Do the 30-second check twice; then do it twice again after you practice lines 7–13.

4 A big smile is worth more than a frown.
5 Type every day with zeal to gain skill.
6 Now is the time to make all your plans.

|1 |2 |3 |4 |5 |6 |7 |8

BUILD SPEED

With practice on down reaches

7 can dim man van ham fan cam lab sac alm
8 slam laces flax scab lack axle land dam
9 band class comma small chalk blank mind
10 seven cant vase ban axle zebra exam lax

|1 |2 |3 |4 |5 |6 |7 |8

D) Use the 5-minute tim-
ing from Lesson 51. Try
to improve your last
score.

52-1.
MEMORANDUM

D) 5-inch line; begin on
line 7. Center MEMO-
RANDUM in all caps;
guide words (DATE, TO,
FROM, SUBJECT) all
caps, left margin. Set
tab stop for 10-space in-
dention for fill-ins. Body
single-spaced, flush left.
Double-space between
paragraphs.

52-2.
UNARRANGED MEMO

D) 5-inch line; tab at 10;
single spacing; start on
line 7.

Listen for your bell to
know when to return
your carriage!

↓7
MEMORANDUM
↓3

DATE   January 2, 19--
                     ↓2
TO   Lori Ann Zoubin

FROM   Alex Torres

SUBJECT   Memos
                     ↓3

Why a memorandum or memo, you ask? Memos can save
time, space, and effort for both the person writing
and the person reading the message. By using the
memo format, one can give a short message a business-
like appearance.

Offices will probably design and use their own special
printed headings for memos. However, for personal
use, the headings given here are appropriate.

                        AT

December 14, 19--; (To) Mrs. Ruth Zenith, Social Chairperson at Goodhaven Nursing Home; (From) Jonathan Doring, Chairperson, Activities
Committee; (Subject) Christmas Party for Residents.

The AMB business chapter is ready to go into action and put on the best
Christmas party ever for the residents of Goodhaven. As you suggested, we
will have the bingo games ready to play at 6 p.m. They will be followed by
a sing-along (song sheets will be distributed to everyone). Punch and
cookies will be served by members of our organization at 9 p.m. We are
looking forward to this annual opportunity to bring Christmas cheer to the
people at Goodhaven.

Who knows—Santa Claus may even arrive!|JD

11 sly ask art rung opera flirt erase jeer
12 just miter aspen went line fly buy disc
13 serve after aster court scar awry pouch

SKILL CHECK

▶ Try to complete this note within 2 minutes and 4 errors. If you can, you are typing 22 words a minute.

14 Dear Bruce: 2
15   3
16   Next week would be a good time for   11
17 us to go to the zoo. We could take our   19
18 picnic and spend the day observing many   27
19 of the animals. I am really interested   35
20 in the more quiet species.   41
21   42
22   James   45
   |1 |2 |3 |4 |5 |6 |7 |8   SI: 1.21

CENTERING TASKS

▶ 18-1. Center vertically on full sheet; center and spread-center lines horizontally as shown; triple-space after first line; double-space the rest.

▶ 18-2. Type a period at edge of line 33 on full sheet; center first 3 lines of 18-1 in upper half and other lines in bottom half.

18-2

GREAT ATHLETES OF THE 1970s

A Special Report By

B A R R Y   C O P P O C K

Submitted To

Mrs. Marian Dechant

Honors English 12

W E S T E R N   H I G H   S C H O O L

Cincinnati, Ohio

October 28, 19--

51-4. ENUMERATION

▶ Center the longest line; tab in four; center on page.

Numbers stand in margin.

Tab in four all lines not starting with a number.

↓3

1. Saute ground chuck; top with sliced green pepper; simmer.

↓2

2. Preheat oven; break greens into salad bowl.

3. Cut bread into small pieces; sprinkle with

cheese; place under broiler until golden.

4. Eat!

SKILL CHECK

▶ Try to type 28 words a minute on a 5-minute timing with 4 or fewer errors.

```
                         1                        2
 5      At a track and field meet, runners race around an oval    12
                     3                        4
 6  track, sprinting toward the finish line.  On a field in the   24
           5                  6                      7
 7  center of this track, other athletes compete for a prize in   36
                        8                 9
 8  throwing contests.  All these games help to make up a track   48
               10                      11                    12
 9  and field meet.  Teams may represent schools, countries, or   60
                       13                       14
10  clubs.  These exciting events are equally well played in or   72
                 15                      16
11  outside; however, the outdoors is preferred for most games.   84
           17                    18                          19
12      Running is probably the oldest form of competition.  A    96
                      20                       21
13  man had to run fast in ancient days to escape from the wild  108
            22                      23                    24
14  beasts.  In self-defense, he had to hurdle obstacles, hoist  120
                         25                     26
15  weights, and climb trees.  Later, man considered these acts  132
                 27                      28
16  of self-defense just as sporting events.                     140
   |1   |2   |3   |4   |5   |6   |7   |8   |9   |10   |11   |12  SI: 1.35
```

52 goals

Type 28 wam on a 5-minute timing. □ Type memorandums.

> **TYPING TIP**
> □ Capitalize a common noun when it is part of a proper name but not when it is used alone in place of the full name:
>
> | Professor Paco | BUT: the professor |
> |---|---|
> | the Iko Corporation | the corporation |
> | Boyle Avenue | the avenue |

WARMUP

Edit as you type.

```
1  Various shoe sizes are still left on the sale shelves here.
2  Her gown was damp hours after she fell into the gusty lake.
3  I addressed the card to 1632 Romer Road; the ZIP was 63409.
4  mrs. zurick was elected president of the olympic committee.
   |1   |2   |3   |4   |5   |6   |7   |8   |9   |10   |11   |12
```

goals

Strengthen control of number keys. ☐ Type 22 wam for 2 minutes within 4 errors on copy with all numbers and letters.

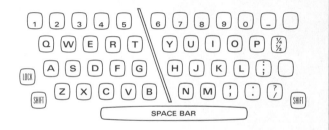

In Lessons 13–18 you learned the reaches for the numbers in the top row of the keyboard. Clinic C, therefore, provides a thorough review of these numbers.

▷ 40-space line; single-space; each line three times or more; double-space between *different* lines.

NUMBER REVIEW

1 frf fr5 f5f 5 55 555 579 853 501 538 55
2 jyj jy6 j6j 6 66 666 648 468 629 926 66
3 frf fr4 f4f 4 44 444 486 648 284 482 44
4 juj ju7 j7j 7 77 777 759 975 207 720 77
5 ded de3 d3d 3 33 333 375 735 301 103 33

6 kik ki8 k8k 8 88 888 846 486 820 208 88
7 sws sw2 s2s 2 22 222 284 824 624 462 22
8 lol lo9 l9l 9 99 999 957 759 295 592 99
9 aqa aq1 a1a 1 11 111 195 591 017 710 11
10 ;p; ;p0 ;0; 0 00 000 037 730 109 910 00

"WE 23" DRILLS

11 we 23 we 23 wet 235 wet 235 wey 236 wey
12 it 85 it 85 pit 085 pit 085 sit 285 sit
13 or 94 or 94 ore 943 ore 943 ort 945 ort

SKILL CHECK

▷ Try to type this note once in 2 minutes (22 wam).

14   You have typed 10, 29, 38, 47, and   8
15 56. Max will quickly check sections 9,   16
16 174, 265, and 839. While he adjusts an   24
17 inventory sheet, please check sizes and   32
18 see if labels are listed. Note changes   40
19 in 56, 59, and 802.   44

|1 |2 |3 |4 |5 |6 |7 |8

SI: 1.25

51

goals

Type 28 wam on a 5-minute timing. ☐ Type poems and numbered lists.

▶ **60-space line; single-space; each line three times or more; double-space between *different* lines.***

* Follow these directions for each one of the Warmup Drills in Unit 9.

WARMUP

1 Exercise those lazy bones daily to stay in a tip-top state.

2 It would seem that October has yet to be the hottest month.

3 Colonel A. Blimp, a newspaper cartoon, was created in 1891.

4 can he name the members of the big ten football conference?

|1 |2 |3 |4 |5 |6 |7 |8 |9 |10 |11 |12

Edit as you type.

51-1. POEM

▶ **Center vertically.**

Type author's name as subtitle *or* as a line under the last verse.

Begin each line with a capital or lowercase letter, following the poet's style.

Set left margin by centering longest line.

                    DEFEAT
                      ↓2
            By James E. Reesnes
                              ↓3

Modern math you've done me in,
 I don't even know where to begin.
My children's homework leaves me cold,
 Oh woe unto me; I feel so old!

51-2. POEM

▶ **Center vertically and horizontally.**

              ATTENTION!
A row of men stood as they should:
)))))))))
I said "Left face!" They understood:
   ((((((((
All but one, who did his best:
                ϒ
But ended facing all the rest:
   (((((((( )
                    --Susan Grant

51-3. POEM

▶ **Select a favorite poem to center.**

goals

To listen for the bell signaling the end of the line. ☐ To type 23 wam for 2 minutes within 4 errors.

▶ **40-space line; single-space; each line three times or more; double-space between** *different* **lines.**

WARMUP

1 zebras quip flaxen mock width joy given
2 The weather is good for the game today.
3 Allow 5 spoiled in each 70 or 9 in 125.

AIM FOR ACCURACY

With practice on: forefinger reaches

4 truth rung my by ugh muff nun funny bun
5 gruff burr furry buy grub hug bunny fry

second-finger reaches

6 kick dice Dick died kicked deeded ceded
7 die, did, iced deed kidded decked diked

third-finger reaches

8 sox loss wool sow slows woos so lox ox.
9 low owls solo wow wools sows ox sol so.

fourth-finger reaches

10 aqua quack zany jazz nap par quick; an?
11 quad qualm quip quiz pay qt. paw prize?

LISTENING FOR YOUR BELL TO KNOW WHEN TO RETURN THE CARRIAGE OR CARRIER

Most of the time when you type from copy or compose your own work you will have to decide when to return the carriage or carrier. That means you must listen for the bell on your typewriter and be ready to finish a line and return the carriage or carrier.

Check your machine—when does the bell ring? Space from the left to the right margin on your machine and note at what point on your scale you hear the bell. How many spaces is that from your desired margin stop? Now remember each time you type a line how many additional spaces you have left to type after you hear your bell ring. You will have to decide how many more letters to type before returning the carriage or carrier.

PART THREE

Now that you have learned how to operate the typewriter well, and how to handle various types of correspondence, you will learn how to handle a variety of reports and related parts of reports.

Part Three consists of four units. Unit 9 (Lessons 51–56) introduces you to the typing of a numbered item, a poem, a memorandum, an outline, a title page, a table of contents, and a bibliography. Unit 10 (Lessons 57–62) teaches you how to format reports that are one page in length. You will learn to type everything from a formal one-page report to a numbered set of directions with a typewriter-drawn map. Unit 11 (Lessons 63–68) expands your skill as you learn to type two-page reports with reference notes. Three different methods of handling reference notes are introduced. You will also learn to use carbon paper. Unit 12 (Lessons 69–74) integrates what you have learned in the other three units. You will learn to complete a full research paper, presented in rough draft form, with a carbon copy.

A Progress Test at the end of the part will allow you to check your understanding and skill in performance of the tasks in Part Three.

When you have completed Part Three, you will be able to:

1. Type 35 words a minute with 4 errors or less.
2. Type a poem, a memo, and an outline in an attractive manner.
3. Arrange a variety of one-page reports in appropriate format.
4. Type a full research paper, which includes a title page, a table of contents, a list of tables, reference notes, a bibliography, and a carbon copy.

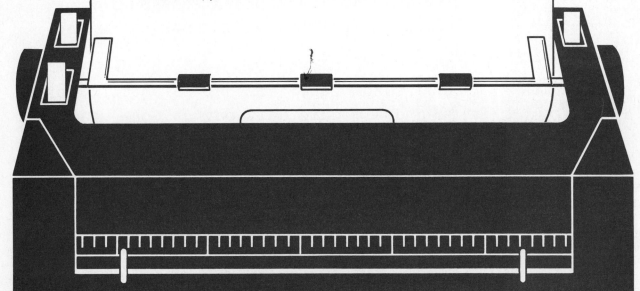

▶ **Set your margins for a 40-space line. As you type each sentence, listen for the bell; without looking up, return your carriage at the point where you think it should be returned. Finish typing the sentence. Then check your return with the key on page 43.**

12 All juniors and seniors must return their library books by May 15.

13 Beginning May 16, a 10-cent per day fee will be charged for books overdue.

14 Any money that is collected for overdue books will be used to buy new ones.

▶ **The exercise below is printed on a 50-space line. Type it on a 40-space line and decide when to end each line.**

SKILL CHECK

▶ Try to type 23 wam for 2 minutes within 4 errors.

15   Every typewriter has pica or elite type. A   10

16 quick check will show which is the size you use.   20

17 With elite type, you get 12 strokes per inch;   29

18 but with pica, you can get just 10. You might   38

19 well do with elite for extra long jobs.   46

|1 |2 |3 |4 |5 |6 |7 |8 |9 |10   **SI: 1.23**

goals

To develop skill in proper word division. ☐ To increase stroking speed and accuracy. ☐ To type 24 wam for 2 minutes within 4 errors.

TYPING TIP
☐ In the same sentence, do not mix constructed fractions (7/8, 5/16) with those that appear on the typewriter (½, ¼).

▶ **40-space line; single-space; each line three times or more; double-space between different lines.**

WARMUP

1 Vi was quite a whiz on mystery puzzles.

2 Jeff learned how to can beets in class.

3 See me at 5 sharp at 639 Second Street.

PENALTY SCALE

−3 Problem is off-center vertically or horizontally.
−3 Line-spacing instruction was not followed.
−3 Words or lines were omitted.
−2 Column entry is out of line.
−2 Paragraph or display line is not indented properly.
−1 Strikeover, incorrect letter or symbol, space omitted, raised capital, or similar typing error.

GRADING SCALE

0–1 = A
2–3 = B
4–6 = C
7–8 = D

PROBLEM 3. PERSONAL LETTER

▶ 50-space line; single spacing. Tab at 5 spaces from left margin and at center. Start on line 13. Use *your own* return address and today's date.

Accumulated production word count is provided after each line of the table, in case you want to determine words-a-minute typed on this production problem. (Production word count takes into consideration machine manipulations such as centering and tabulating.)

Dear George:	3
Your letter telling us that you will be able	13
to visit our farm during the first three weeks of	23
July is wonderful news. Here are some activities	43
we are planning for you:	48
1. You will learn to milk the cows.	56
2. You will go to a chicken barbecue on	65
July 4; there will be hog calling and dancing.	75
3. There are several lakes nearby where we	85
will swim and water ski.	90
4. We have a fish pond that is well stocked	100
with bass. You will have a chance to go fishing.	110
5. Of course, you will have the opportunity	120
to take part in haymaking!	126
We are looking forward to your visit.	135
See you soon,	140

|1 |2 |3 |4 |5 |6 |7 |8 |9 |10 **SI: 1.32**

SKILL CHECK

▶ Try to type 30 words per minute with 4 or fewer errors.

1 Do you realize how many people began to water ski 10
2 in recent years? The sport provides exercise for 20
3 all ages--from young to old. Water skiing is for 30
4 summer what snow skiing is for winter. Skiing is 40
5 an exercise in good balance. Those with adequate 50
6 skill may use just one ski; others will wear both 60
7 skis. To water ski, one needs to have a tow boat 70
8 with a strong enough engine to pull the skier out 80
9 of the water. Ski shows are given in the summer. 90

|1 |2 |3 |4 |5 |6 |7 |8 |9 |10 **SI: 1.31**

4 common occur off need effect assist err

5 manner puppy inn buff occupy career zoo

6 cannot happy ill room summer degree too

7 purse fifth today look would diet types

8 wheat ideas apply help other work study

9 yeast hired treat plow paper just poets

RULES FOR WORD DIVISION

Absolute Rules

1. Divide only between whole syllables. If uncertain where a syllable ends, check in a dictionary. Some words can be difficult—it is *ser-vice* and not *serv-ice*.

2. Carry to a second line a syllable of at least (a) 3 letters or (b) 2 letters and a punctuation mark, and leave a syllable of at least 2 letters on the upper line. Thus *de-tract* and *there-of,* but not *a-fire* or *bus-y.*

3. Do not divide a word pronounced as one syllable (*trimmed*), any contraction (*doesn't*), or any abbreviation (*Ph.D.* or *f.o.b.*).

Preferential Rules

1. If two accented vowels occur together, divide between them. For example, *valu-able* is preferred to *valua-ble.*

2. If a one-letter syllable occurs in the middle of a word, divide after the letter. Thus *simi-lar* is better than *sim-ilar.*

3. Divide compounds either where they are normally hyphenated or at the point where two words join to make a solid compound. For example, *get-together* is better than *get-to-gether.* (Do not add an extra hyphen.) Divide solid compounds between the separate words. For example, *home-owner* is better than *home-own-er.*

4. Avoid breaking prefixes and suffixes. Divide a word after the prefix rather than within the prefix. For example, *circum-stance* is preferred to *cir-cumstance.* Divide a word before the suffix rather than within the suffix. Thus *forc-ible* is better than *forci-ble.*

WORD DIVISION PRACTICE

▷ Select from the three columns the word that is divided according to the rules reviewed above. (Check your answers on page 44.)

	a.	b.	c.
10	passed	pas-sed	pass-ed
11	a-mount	amount	am-ount
12	dim-ple	dimp-le	di-mple
13	lett-er	le-tter	let-ter
14	super-vision	su-pervision	supervi-sion
15	criti-cal	crit-ical	cri-tical
16	timeta-ble	time-table	timetab-le
17	valuab-le	valua-ble	valu-able
18	in-troduce	int-roduce	intro-duce
19	double-spac- ing	double- spacing	dou- ble-spacing
20	extra-ordinary	ex-traordinary	extraor-dinary

Key to exercise on page 42. Line 12 should end with *their.* Line 13 should end with *fee.* Line 14 should end with *overdue.*

part two progress test

goals

Type reference card. ☐ Type table from rough draft copy. ☐ Type personal letter with numbered list.

▶ **There are four parts to this test. Each reviews what you have been learning since Lesson 26. Follow the directions given for each specific problem.**

PROBLEM 1. REFERENCE CARD, 4″ x 6″

▶ This is a library reference card written for a term paper. Cut paper to size and type the card in proper form.

> Book, William F.
>
> <u>Learning to Typewrite.</u> New York, The Gregg Publishing Company, 1925, 451 pages.
>
> A complete presentation of the acquisition of typewriting skill as viewed in the early 1920s. The book is written for the teacher of typewriting. Divided into three parts, the book deals with the topics of: (1) The Psychology of Skill and Laws which Govern its Acquisition in Typewriting, (2) Scientific Analysis of Learning to Typewrite, and (3) The Role of the Teacher in Selecting and Directing Learners of Typewriting.

PROBLEM 2. TABULATION IN ROUGH DRAFT

▶ Double-space; set margin and tab stops; make all corrections as indicated.

BASKETBALL SCHEDULE

The Orfordville Vikings

<u>Dates</u>	<u>Opponent</u>	<u>Play</u>	<u>Time</u>
Nov. 10	Baraboo	Home	7:00
Nov. 17	Evansville	Away	3:30
Nov. 24	Juda	Home	7:00
Dec. 2	Edgerton	Home 7:00	
Dec. 9	St. Paul's	Away	7:30
Dec. 16	~~Oregon~~ Verona	Away	~~6:00~~ 7:00
Dec. 28	Middleton	Home	7:00
Jan. 4	Mt. Clemens	Away	8:00
Jan. 12	Beloit	away	2:30
Jan. 19	Sussex	Home	7:00

SKILL CHECK

▶ 40-space line; double spacing; listen for the bell. If you type correctly, all lines will end evenly. Try to type 24 wam for 2 minutes within 4 errors.

21 Just back in the last lesson, you found that 9
22 there are two kinds of type--elite and 17
23 pica. Each one, however, takes the same 25
24 six spaces up and down to make one inch. 33
25 Each size can give a top-quality result 41
26 to all the papers you will type. 48
|1 |2 |3 |4 |5 |6 |7 |8 |9 SI: 1.21

goals

To increase stroking speed and accuracy. To learn the # , $, %, &, ¢, @, and * keys. □ To type 25 wam for 2 minutes within 4 errors.

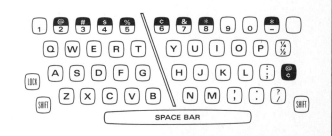

▶ **40-space line; single-space; each line three times or more; double-space between *different* lines.**

WARMUP

1 wax spa jug nod eve fir why zap elk mob
2 and say who rib fog lens pane chap wish
3 We demand a 3 by 4, 10-foot-long board.

BUILD SPEED

With practice on down reaches

4 jobs flax back wave ping crab jibe many
5 next mind cast pack webs pen hung class
6 bubble smell think thing save sang calm
7 along blaze vague bark scrub pond maxim
|1 |2 |3 |4 |5 |6 |7 |8

AIM FOR ACCURACY

With practice on consecutive finger strokes

8 debate stroke just loam frogs sold zany
9 must grade zany trot long fort defy low
10 minute program grassy swoop lower sweat
11 swamp frail forth edit delay lodge love

Key to exercise on page 43. 10. **a** 11. **b** 12. **a** 13. **c** 14. **a** 15. **a** 16. **b** 17. **c** 18. **c** 19. **b** 20. **a**

1. From Anne Bauer, typing teacher, Lincoln High School. The school offers two semesters of typing; a student may elect to take only the first semester; she estimates that 84 percent of the students who graduate do have some typewriting experience.

2. From Lester Bell, Wantagh High School, typing instructor. They offer one semester of personal typing as well as two semesters of vocational typing; he estimates that 95 percent of the students who graduate have enrolled in a typing course.

3. From Gene Spana, Jefferson High School, business education teacher. His school offers one semester of personal typing to all students from freshmen through seniors, and four semesters of vocational typewriting for those who wish additional skill; he estimates that 90 percent of the students who graduate will have been enrolled in a course in typing.

4. From Marty Gross, typing teacher, Central High School. His school offers one semester of personal typing along with two more of vocational typing; he adds the note that this is a very small school and most students are advised to take typing before leaving school; therefore, almost 100 percent of the students have typing skill before graduation.

49-2. TABLE

Your survey is now completed and you need to summarize your data. Type this table that will show the percent of students who take some typing instruction before graduation.

Type the high schools in alphabetic order.

SUMMARY OF SURVEY ON TYPEWRITING) *D. S.*
19--

Name of School	Percent Who Take Typing
Lincoln	84
Trinity	90
Jefferson	90
Wantagh	95
Central	100
Mumford	80
Visitation	~~95~~ *90*
Jackson	88

) S. S.

Compose a short questionnaire that you will type on a slip of paper postcard size, or on a half sheet of paper. The questionnaire is to be distributed to all students in your class. This topic is suggested: find out if students hold a part-time job, the hours they work, the total hours per week, and a short description of the job. Compose the questionnaire and set it up in good form.

▶ Practice these sentences. You previewed the words in lines 4–11 on p. 44.

12 A blaze by the pond cast webs of smoke.

13 A backlog of jobs is the thing to save.

14 A crab sang his song in the back ponds.

|1 |2 |3 |4 |5 |6 |7 |8

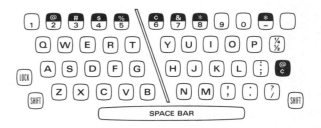

▶ Select the appropriate finger for symbols $, #, %, &, ¢, @, and *. 40-space line; single spacing; tab 5; each line three times; double-space between *different* lines.

NEW SYMBOLS

$ Use F finger.
#   Use D finger.
%   Use F finger.
&   Use J finger.

15 Use the dollar sign, $, before numbers.

16 Use the number sign, #, before figures.

17 Use the percent sign, %, after figures.

18 This sign, &, is the ampersand, or and.

Manual	Electric
¢ Sem Finger	J Finger
@ Sem Finger	S Finger
* Sem Finger	K Finger

19 The cents symbol, ¢, is used for money.

20 This symbol, @, means the rate charged.

21 The star or asterisk, *, marks an item.

NEW KEY REINFORCEMENT

22   The keys on which @, ¢, and * will

23 be found depend on the make of machine,

24 but #, $, %, and & are always the same.

SKILL CHECK

▶ Try to type 25 wam for 2 minutes within 4 errors.

25   Learning to type is fun. But more   8

26 important is that typing will be a most   16

27 useful tool all your life. You have to   24

28 feel sorry for a person who types using   32

29 just one finger from each hand. As you   40

30 acquire more skill, typing a paper will   48

31 be a snap.   50

|1 |2 |3 |4 |5 |6 |7 |8   SI: 1.24

goals

Type 30 wam on a 3-minute timing. ☐
Compose postcards. ☐
Increase skill in typing tables.

◗ 50-space line; single-space; each line three times or more; double-space between *different* lines.

WARMUP

1 It is inexcusable to become lax and weak in work.

2 One semester of typing will give skill to retain.

3 Samo (my dog) had fleas—for the first time ever.

Insert missing letters.

4 T-e alg-br- test w-s hard b-t I th--k I d-d w-l-.
   |1 |2 |3 |4 |5 |6 |7 |8 |9 |10

BUILD SPEED

With practice on double letter words.

5 bb ebb ebbs abbot rubbed clubbed drubbed dribbled

6 mm dimmer summer mammoth shimmer stammer simmered

7 nn dinner banner spinner innings manners winnings

8 ss lesson assess missing session classic missiles

9 oo sooner doomed cooking coolers crooked crooning
   |1 |2 |3 |4 |5 |6 |7 |8 |9 |10

SKILL CHECK

◗ Try to type 30 words a minute in a 3-minute timing with 4 or fewer errors.

10   Sailing is an exciting water sport. Numbers   10

11 are drawn to the thrills of sailing a boat as the   20

12 strong breezes stir bodies of waters in all parts   30

13 of the world. Sailboats range in size from small   40

14 dinghies to large yachts that can cross an ocean.   50

15 Quite a few people enjoy competing in a race with   60

16 crafts of different kinds.   65

17   Some of the sailboats have hulls formed from   75

18 wooden planking fastened over the frame. Current   85

19 boats use more fiberglass.   90
    |1 |2 |3 |4 |5 |6 |7 |8 |9 |10   **SI: 1.33**

22

goals

To learn the reach for the apostrophe (') and quotation ('') keys. □ To type 25 wam for 2 minutes within 4 errors.

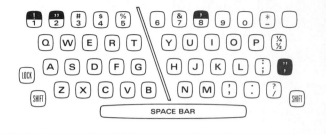

▶ **40-space line; single-space; each line three times or more; double-space between *different* lines.**

1 swat boxed ooze every stump scent juicy

2 pride whale fish own also got did sharp

3 Kate quickly sent 4 boxes @ $1.50 each.

▶ **Select the appropriate drill for your machine. 40-space line; single spacing; each line three times; double-space between *different* lines.**

APOSTROPHE KEY

Manual—Use K finger.

Electric—Use Sem finger.

If the exclamation mark is on the number 1 key, practice line 6 using the A finger.

To make the exclamation mark (line 6), type a period, backspace, then type an apostrophe.

4 k8k k'k k8k k'k It's your turn to lead.

5 ;'; ;'; ''' ;'; It's your turn to lead.

6 a!a a!a !a! !a! Alas! No! Yes! Heavens!

7 I've had enough of Kelly's humor today!

8 The student's test wasn't done on time.

9 Didn't the cat's eyes glow in the dark?

QUOTATION KEY

Manual—Use S finger.

Electric—Use Sem finger.

10 s2s s"s s2s s"s I said, "See you soon."

11 ;'; ;"; ;'; ;"; I said, "See you soon."

The quotation mark always *follows* a comma and a period but always *precedes* a colon and a semicolon. The quotation mark *follows* a question mark or an exclamation point IF the quoted words are actually a question or an exclamation. If they are not, the quotation mark *precedes* the punctuation.

NEW KEY REINFORCEMENT

12 Betty's only reaction to it was "When?"

13 I yelled, "Help!" "Witty" is the word.

14 "Wow, what a blazing fire!" he shouted.

15 It's my sister's turn to do the dishes.

16 The word "badger" has several meanings.

17 "Will you try to type more accurately?"

▶ Type four extra copies of the card for use in the next lesson. (Use a photocopier to make copies if one is available.)

```
        Number of semesters of typewriting offered in
        my school:  _____

        Approximate percentage of students who take
        typing in my school is: _____

        Additional comments:  _____

        _____

        _____

             NAME  _____

             NAME OF HIGH SCHOOL  _____
```

SKILL CHECK

▶ Try to type 30 words a minute in a 3-minute timing with 4 or fewer errors.

```
10        Skiing is the exciting sport of zipping over    10
11   slopes with deep snow while wearing boards called    20
12   skis.  Persons from almost all parts of the world    30
13   enjoy the thrill of skimming over the snow.  Most    40
14   of the big ski resorts have the equipment for all    50
15   types of skiers, including many chair lifts.        59
16        Skiing as a sport began in the early days of    69
17   this country and became part of the Olympic Games    79
18   in 1924.  It was in France that winter games were   89
19   held.                                               90

     |1    |2    |3    |4    |5    |6    |7    |8    |9    |10   SI: 1.32
```

SKILL CHECK

▶ Try to type 25 wam for 2 minutes within 4 errors.

18	Among the greatest aims in schools	8
19	is for you to express ideas in writing.	16
20	If you can organize your thoughts while	24
21	at the typewriter, it is much better to	32
22	jot down your view with type. You will	40
23	quickly form good skill at this task by	48
24	hard work.	50

goals

To learn the reach for the parenthesis ( ) keys, the underscore _ key, the + and = keys. □ To type 25 wam for 2 minutes within 4 errors.

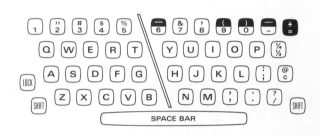

▶ 40-space line; single-space; tab 5; each line three times or more; double-space between *different* lines.

WARMUP

1 quote realize empty buzz knee wave taxi
2 apt end ham fig envy joy clad talk hand
3 Sue took 3, 5, 7, and 9 in the drawing.

PARENTHESIS KEYS

Use shifts of 9 and 0 keys.

4 191 1(1 191 1(1 ;0; ;); ;0; (a) (1) (4)
5 Choose (a) good; (b) fair; or (c) poor.
6 Becky (the hostess) has been very busy.
7 Number this with (1), (2), (3), or (4).

UNDERSCORE KEY

Manual—Use J finger.

Electric—Use Sem finger.

Type the word, backspace, and underscore it immediately.

8 j6j j_j j6j j_j He <u>did</u> say that to her.
8 ;−; ;_; ;−; ;_; He <u>did</u> say that to her.

A. Business Letter, 145 words in body. Tab at center; single-space; begin typing on line 13. Type your own name in the signature line.
B. Envelope, large or small.
C. Card to enclose with letter. Refer to the illustration on p. 93 to type the postcard.

(School name
and address)
Current date
↓5

Mr. Elvin Seymour
Business Education Department
Mumford High School
497 Midmoor Road
Bluebell, UT 84007
↓2

Dear Mr. Seymour:
↓2

Our class in personal typing had a discussion recently concerning the number of students who take typing in their high school course of study. All members of our class are enthusiastic about the merits of typing, and we feel that everyone should learn to type.

Miss Iona, our typing teacher, has asked me to contact several business education teachers to make a survey on how many semesters of typing are offered by schools and how many students take typing before graduation. You are one of the teachers in my survey. Would you please help me obtain this information by filling out the enclosed card and returning it to me as soon as possible?

If you would like a summary of the findings, please add a note to that effect on your return card.
↓2

                    Sincerely,
                              ↓4

                    Heather Krist
                              ↓2

Enclosure

+ ≡ KEY

Electric—Use Sem finger.
Manual—Use A finger.

NEW KEY REINFORCEMENT
Review ( ), _, +, and =.

SKILL CHECK

▷ Try to type 25 wam for 2 minutes within 4 errors.

9 We have read the book <u>Pay Up, Mr. Paul</u>.
10 <u>No</u> <u>person</u> is to help you with the test!
11 The underscore may be used for <u>emphasis</u>.

12 ;=; === ;=; === A = 26, B = 37, C = 48.
13 ;=; ;=+ ;+; ;+; 6 + 17 + 23 + 58 = 104.
14 Frank, how much is a + 173 if a = 6780?
15 Yes, 16 + 16 = 32, but what is 32 + 16?

16 I was tired (but not exhausted) Monday.
17 Did they ever hear the opera <u>La Boheme</u>?
18 95 = A, 87 = B, 78 = C, 70 = D, 60 = F.
19 102 (51 + 51) + 898 (449 + 449) = 1000.

20   An author of novels who was unable   8
21 to type set aside a six-month period to   16
22 learn the skill. Once he had developed   24
23 the skill to type quite well, he seized   32
24 on the thought of writing all his books   40
25 with a machine. He enjoys the hours he   48
26 can save.   50

|1 |2 |3 |4 |5 |6 |7 |8   SI: 1.26

goals

To increase stroking speed and accuracy. □ To construct new symbols. □ To type 25 wam for 2 minutes within 4 errors.

TYPING TIP
□ Underscore titles of books, pamphlets, long poems, magazines, and newspapers. Also underscore titles of movies, musicals, operas, paintings, and pieces of sculpture.

▷ **40-space line; single-space; each line three times or more; double-space between *different* lines.**

WARMUP

1 The prize on solving the puzzle is big!
2 cog few love then snake many sandy busy
3 Find the apostrophe ('); quotation (").

SKILL CHECK

▶ Try to type 30 words a minute in a 3-minute timing with 4 or fewer errors.

8   Skin diving is another term for free diving.   10
9 Skin divers explore the world beneath the surface   20
10 of hazy oceans, lakes, and deep streams.   28
11   The most simple form of skin diving is to go   38
12 under water while holding one's breath. This can   48
13 be done without any equipment. Most skin divers,   58
14 though, who hold their breath under water, do use   68
15 rubber foot fins and see through a face mask. By   78
16 the use of a metal air tank, a deeper dive can be   88
17 enjoyed.   90

|1 |2 |3 |4 |5 |6 |7 |8 |9 |10   **SI: 1.33**

goals

Type 30 wam on a 3-minute timing. □ Build skill in typing a personal letter, an envelope, and a postcard.

TYPING TIP
□ When *Jr.*, *Sr.*, or a roman numeral—such as *III*—is typed after a name, omit the comma before *Jr.*, *Sr.*, or the roman numeral unless you know that the person addressed prefers the use of a comma.

▶ **50-space line; single-space; Type each line three times or more; double-space between *different* lines.**

WARMUP

1 The cave dweller was a recluse--exiled from life.
2 Silver lakes and rocky dells are beautiful mates.
3 We need 5 ads @ $13.75 each to break even for it.

Insert vowels.

4 Calico c-ts w-r- pl-ced -n the b-x t- be sh-pp-d.

|1 |2 |3 |4 |5 |6 |7 |8 |9 |10

BUILD SPEED

With practice on double letters

5 ee see free bleed sleepy meeting feeding sheepish
6 ll all full alley mellow bellman speller collared
7 rr terror horrid married terrier corrals hurrying
8 pp happen pepper shipped flipped suppers supports
9 zz razzle dazzle fizzles guzzled sizzles drizzled

4 Chapter VIII of <u>Living America</u> is good.
5 The <u>sum</u> of 0, 9, 17, 23, 48, 56 is 153.
6 It's Sandy's turn to wash mother's car.
7 He couldn't say, "It's Bo's new glove."
8 Vic (the captain) caught the long pass.
9 I checked items (1), (5), (8), and (9).
10 Do you talk with "I" and "me" too much?
11 "Well, hello," Dick said, "come on in."

▶ 30-SECOND SPEED CHECK

12 Do not let the bark of the dogs bother,   8
13 nor the meow of cats pierce your sleep.   16

|1 |2 |3 |4 |5 |6 |7 |8

CONSTRUCTING SYMBOLS

Knowing how to construct special symbols will be useful for anyone who must prepare a term paper on a topic of a technical nature or a paper that presents statistical data. The following sentences explain how to construct special symbols and provide examples of their use.

▶ Type each line until you feel you have mastered the symbols involved.

14 The small x (s finger) conveys "times."
15 26 x 2 equals 52.
16 The hyphen is a minus or subtract sign.
17 25 − 10 equals 15.
18 26 x 2 − 10 = 42
19 Put a colon over a hyphen for division.
20 39 ÷ 13 = 3

AIM FOR ACCURACY

With practice on x, q, p, and z

21 The next exit exists at the Exiam Apex.
22 Quickly quote the quite popular quotes.
23 Please pay a tip upon payment of paint.
24 A zero on my quiz zaps the zip from me.

BUILD SPEED

With practice on down reaches

25 Men or women can take care of the home.
26 An honest inner feeling came over them.
27 A beehive of activities existed before.
28 Make the best of each new chance given.

goals

Type 30 wam on a 3-minute timing. ☐
Compose a table. ☐
Type a table from rough-draft copy.

▷ **50-space line; single-space; each line three times or more; double-space between** *different* **lines.**

WARMUP

1 His quick wit exemplifies his breezy way of life.

2 Her sweet tooth demands candy every now and then.

3 There were 9 cats, 6 dogs, 2 goats, and 1 parrot.

Insert missing letters.

4 Rust c–n quic–ly d–ll th– finish –f y––r new ca–.

|1 |2 |3 |4 |5 |6 |7 |8 |9 |10

LONGHAND SPRINT

▷ Try to type rapidly from longhand.

5 Car pooling stopped when Meagen sold her old car.

6 The salary scale for the file clerks will change.

7 The representative will visit foreign lands next.

▷ **47-1. COMPOSING A TABLE**

Ms. Marneffe responds to your letter (Task 46-2) in which you requested information on the courses offered in the English Department during the summer session. Arrange and type a table that will show the courses offered and the day and time. Use appropriate column headings.

World Literature—MWF, 8:00–10:00; American Literature, 1600–1900—MWF, 11:00–1:00; American Literature, 1900–Present—MWF, 2:00–4:00; Shakespeare—TTh, 8:00–10:00; Modern British Literature—TTh, 11:00–1:00; Medieval Literature—TTh, 2:00–4:00; Early Chaucer—TTh, 4:00–6:00

47-2. TABLE WITH MONEY COLUMNS

▷ 4 columns with headings; full sheet; single-space body of table.

PRESS CLUB RECEIPTS FOR FALL

Date of Newspaper	Subscriptions	Advertisements	Total
Oct. 1	$ 25.00	$ 40.00	$ 65.00
Oct. 15	25.00	40.00	65.00
Nov. 1	23.00	40.00	63.00
Nov. 15	26.00	42.50	68.50
Dec. 1	30.00	45.00	75.00
Total	$129.00	$207.50	$336.50

If you are practicing all of these new symbols at one time, perhaps you will want to take a break after line 31.

29 "Divided into" symbol is built with the
30 right parenthesis and some underscores.
31 $20 \overline{)\ 9040} = 452$
32 Turn cylinder a half line down to make:
33 $a^2\ b^2\ c^2$
34 Turn cylinder about a half line up for:
35 H_2O
36 A caret is one underscore and diagonal.
        ever
37 Aim/higher
38 Diagonals and underscores facing inward
39 will make a bracket.
40 /turn to page 61./
41 Use an apostrophe to construct feet and
42 minutes.
43 6' or 6 feet; 20' or 20 minutes
44 Use the quotation mark to make the sign
45 for inches and seconds.
46 2" or 2 inches; 12" or 12 seconds
47 To show a ratio, use one or two colons.
48 1:4::2:X = 8

SKILL CHECK

▶ Try to type 25 wam or more in 2 minutes within 4 errors.

49   One must stress the great worth of   8
50 practice as you learn to type. Just to   16
51 type is not a good enough aim. Posture   24
52 at the machine plus typing with a fixed   32
53 objective are required in working for a   40
54 triumph of the keyboard. Zeal and will   48
55 can help.   50

|1 |2 |3 |4 |5 |6 |7 |8   SI: 1.23

ACCURACY OR
SPEED PRACTICE

SKILL CHECK

▶ Try to type 29 words a minute in a 3-minute timing with 4 or fewer errors.

▶ Type the drills appropriate for you from Lesson 32, p. 65: lines 10–13 for accuracy or lines 14–17 for speed.

5 Soccer is one of the most approved sports in   10
6 the world. In many countries of the world, it is   20
7 the national sport. Teams of 11 try to knock the   30
8 round ball through the opponent's goal. The game   40
9 is tough, zealous, exciting. It demands strength   50
10 of physique, since play goes on without stopping.   60
11 Time is called only when a goal is scored, a foul   70
12 is made, or a player is injured. The play period   80
13 per game is one hour and one-half.   87

|1 |2 |3 |4 |5 |6 |7 |8 |9 |10   **SI: 1.27**

▶ **46-1. Business Letter and Large Envelope.** 120 words in body; indent paragraphs 5 spaces.

Today's date ↓5 | Mr. Fred Bahr | 2390 Woodlawn Avenue | Dorloo, NY 12099 | Dear Mr. Bahr: |

Thank you for participating in our on-campus day March 1. Indeed, it was a pleasure to meet with you, your sister, and Mr. Pinero to answer your questions and concerns about college life.

As I promised, I am enclosing a copy of the brochure that will further explain the programs we discussed together. An Application for Admission form is also enclosed as you had requested.

Please contact me whenever I might be of help to you. We are looking forward to receiving your completed application form and welcoming you to McIntyre College. Perhaps in another year we will have the pleasure of welcoming your sister, Rita, to our institution. | Sincerely yours, | Arlisle Marneffe | Admissions Office | urs | Enclosures

▶ **46-2. Composing a Personal Business Letter and Large Envelope.** Indent paragraphs 5 spaces. Judge the number of words in your letter before deciding on the correct margin sets.

Write a letter to Ms. Marneffe, thanking her for the brochure you received that further explained the program you will pursue at McIntyre College. Also tell her you have completed the form, Application for Admission, and are enclosing it with the letter. You have decided to begin your freshman course work this summer. Request information on the courses offered in the English Department during the summer session.

(Refer back to Lesson 32, p. 66, to review the steps in composing.)

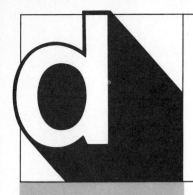

goal

To strengthen control of symbol keys.

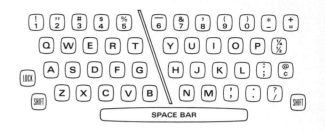

▶ **40-space line; single-space; each line three times or more; double-space between *different* lines.**

In Lessons 19–24, you completed your study of the keyboard by learning the special symbol keys and how to construct symbols not on the keyboard. Clinic D reviews your skill with the special symbols.

REVIEW OF ALL
SYMBOLS

1 I held our 1¢, 10¢, 25¢, and 50¢ coins.
2 First @ .10, second @ .20, third @ .30.
3 Type the stars: 211* and 415* and 523*
4 "Mert" and "Dick" and "Betsy" are pups.
5 I'll go if it's for the Winners' Party.
6 191 1(1 ;0; ;); (9) (10) (34) (192) (1)

▶ **30-SECOND
SPEED CHECK**

7 The pups (only 2 months old) are "blue—   8
8 ribbon" and should sell for a price @ ?   16

|1 |2 |3 |4 |5 |6 |7 |8

▶ **Use directions
for Warmup.**

9 <u>Please</u> do not take my <u>Bingo Verse Book</u>.
10 Is 16:1::20:5? Is 15:5::30:10? Which?
11 It would be great! Meet me at 8 sharp!
12 Grade of A, 93%; B, 86%; C, 78%; D, 70%
13 Sell crates #213 first; next sell #419.
14 I have given $9, $15, $26, $32, and $1.
15 25 & 27 & 35 & 49 & 60 & 78 & 172 & 196
16 2 + 3 + 5 + 7 + 8 + 11 + 14 + 169 + 183
17 One = A; 2 = B; 3 = C; 4 = D; 5 = Fail.

▶ **30-SECOND
SPEED CHECK**

18 Under <u>D</u> for <u>diamond</u>, find the % and $'s   8
19 controlled by Ret & Co. Bet it's huge!   16

|1 |2 |3 |4 |5 |6 |7 |8

```
Mr. Fred Bahr
2390 Woodlawn Avenue
Dorloo, NY 12099



                Ms. Arlisle Marneffe
                Admissions Office
                McIntyre College
                500 Main Street
                Tulsa, OK 74112
```

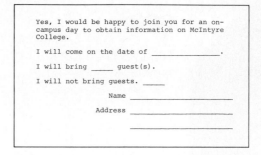

```
Yes, I would be happy to join you for an on-
campus day to obtain information on McIntyre
College.

I will come on the date of _____.

I will bring _____ guest(s).

I will not bring guests. _____

                Name _____

             Address _____

                  _____
```

▶ **45-2. Personal Letter and Small Envelope. 80 words in body; indent paragraphs 5 spaces.**

Using your own home address, type the following letter: Return address, line 13 | Today's date ↓5 | Ms. Arlisle Marneffe | Admissions Office | McIntyre College | 500 Main Street | Tulsa, OK 74112 | Dear Ms. Marneffe: |

Thank you very much for inviting me to your campus. As indicated on my enclosed card, I have selected the date of March 1 to visit your college.

My parents will not be able to accompany me on this date, but my teacher, Mr. Pinero, would like to visit your campus. My sister, who is a junior in high school, is interested in attending your college when she graduates, so she will be coming, too. | Sincerely, | your name | enclosure

▶ **45-3. Fill in the return postcard to enclose with the letter you typed in Task 45-2. Use your own name and home return address.**

46

goals

Type 29 wam on a 3-minute writing. ☐ Increase skill in typing and composing letters, and typing envelopes.

TYPING TIPS
☐ On a one-page letter, leave a bottom margin of at least six lines, and preferably of nine lines.
☐ On a two-page letter, the bottom margin on the first page can be increased up to twelve lines.

▶ **50-space line; single-space; each line three times or more; double-space between *different* lines.**

WARMUP

1 If you are anxious, inquire or seek help quickly.
2 Let me live in the house by the side of the road.
3 If he has 1235 or 1259, I will take 1268 or 1274.
4 Th-y g-t the j-bs beca-se -f th--r t-p-ng sk-lls.

Insert missing letters.

```
|1    |2    |3    |4    |5    |6    |7    |8    |9    |10
```

part one progress test

goals

Type 25 wam for 2 minutes within 4 errors.
☐ Center and block center items vertically and horizontally.

TYPING TIPS
☐ When you block-center, all the lines are even at the left margin.
☐ When you spread-center, leave 1 space between letters and 2 spaces between words.

The first section of this test consists of two 2-minute skill checks.

▷ **40-space line; double-space; 5-space paragraph indention for each of the timings.**

STRAIGHT COPY SKILL CHECK

1 Did you think that coed sports had	8
2 their start in this century? A look at	16
3 croquet shows us that coed sports had a	24
4 start much sooner. Croquet won fame as	32
5 the first sport played in the U.S.A. by	40
6 both sexes. Just imagine how amazing a	48
7 discovery.	50

|1 |2 |3 |4 |5 |6 |7 |8   SI: 1.37

NUMBER/SYMBOL SKILL CHECK

8 Since 1786 teams have been zinging	8
9 balls through 9 wickets and 2 stakes to	16
10 top the score. As few as 2 or 3 (or 4,	24
11 5, or 6) can play the game. The object	32
12 is to go through all the wickets and to	40
13 hit both stakes without being "sent out	48
14 of sight."	50

|1 |2 |3 |4 |5 |6 |7 |8   SI: 1.19

The second section of this test consists of two centering tasks. Above the tasks is a penalty scale for any errors on the tasks. By applying the penalty to the grading scale, you can determine your grade for each task.

goals

Type 29 wam for 3 minutes within 4 errors.
☐ Increase skill in typing letters and cards.

TYPING TIP
☐ If it is necessary to conserve space on a postcard, the salutation can be omitted.

▷ **50-space line; single-space; each line three times or more; double-space between *different* lines.**

WARMUP

1 Gingerly shake the hot coals away from the vents.

2 Winds do howl but snowflakes fall in silent form.

3 My typing mistakes went from 15 to 13 to 10 to 8.

Insert letters.

4 My ent—re proj—ct —s just about re—dy f—r ty—ing.
   |1 |2 |3 |4 |5 |6 |7 |8 |9 |10

ACCURACY OR SPEED PRACTICE

▷ **Type the drills appropriate for you in Lesson 32, p. 65: lines 6–9 for accuracy or lines 10–13 for speed.**

SKILL CHECK

▷ Try to type 29 words a minute in a 3-minute timing with 4 or fewer errors.

5 Stadiums in which athletic events take place   10

6 have grown in size, cost, and luxury to all. The   20

7 first stadium to be enclosed was the Astrodome in   30

8 Houston. This structure was built to protect the   40

9 players and the fans from unpleasant weather.   49

10   The stadium in Denver is unique since one of   59

11 its sides (weighing 9 million pounds) can be slid   69

12 out to make room to play other sports. This is a   79

13 jubilant feat of know—how and skills.   87
   |1 |2 |3 |4 |5 |6 |7 |8 |9 |10 SI: 1.35

POSTCARDS

A postcard measures 5½″ x 3¼″. The centering point is 2¾″ (27 pica spaces or 33 elite) from the edge. The card has 19 lines of typing space. Deducting ½″ for each side margin will leave 4½″ for typing (45 pica spaces or 54 elite).

▷ **45-1. A postcard is to be enclosed with the letter you typed in Task 44-1. A miniature of the card is shown on p. 88. On a slip of paper cut to 5½″ x 3¼″ or an actual postcard, type the message in proper form.**

−3   problem is off center vertically or horizontally

−3   line-spacing instruction was not followed

−3   words or lines were omitted

−2   display line is not centered

−1   strikeover, incorrect letter or symbol, space omitted, raised capital, or similar typing error

BLOCK CENTERING

▶ **Center vertically and block-center the following item on a half sheet of paper; go down three lines after the title; double-space the rest of the lines.**

R O Q U E

Roque is a game that is not very well known. It is a form of croquet that is played in leagues in the United States. Roque is played on a court that has a hard surface. The court measures 50 by 100 feet. Ten wickets are placed at various places on the court. Points are scored by passing the ball through a wicket and by hitting a stake. It takes 16 points to win a game.

CENTERING

▶ **Center vertically and horizontally the following announcement on a full sheet of paper; go down three lines after the title; double-space the rest of the lines. Type each line as shown.**

Y O U   A R E   I N V I T E D

To Participate

in the

ANNUAL ROQUE TOURNAMENT

Sunday, July 28, 19--

at 3:00 p.m.

Willow Grove Park

ENTRY DEADLINE: June 14

Estimated No. of Words in Body	Line Length
Under 100	4 inches (40 pica, 50 elite spaces)
100–200	5 inches (50 pica, 60 elite spaces)
Over 200	6 inches (60 pica, 70 elite spaces)

Use this table to determine line length for your letters.

▷ **44-1. Business Letter and Large (No. 10) Envelope. 197 words in body. 5-inch line; single-spacing; tab at center; 5-space paragraph indent. Begin letterhead on line 7 and date on line 15.**

McINTYRE COLLEGE

500 Main Street

Tulsa, OK 74112

(Current Date)
↓5

Mr. Fred Bahr
2390 Woodlawn Avenue
Dorloo, NY 12099

Dear Mr. Bahr:

    Your guidance counselor has let us know that you have shown an interest in attending a four-year college after you graduate from high school. Mr. Joseph Markowitz said that you are interested in McIntyre College.

    In order to provide you with the very best information on the type of programs we offer, we have established four on-campus days. These days provide you with the opportunity to see our campus and visit with faculty. The dates this year are October 14, December 17, February 4, and March 1. We would like to invite you and your parents to visit us on one of these dates and obtain information on our programs, degrees, campus activities, dorm accommodations, and so on.

    Please complete the enclosed card indicating the date you would prefer to visit our campus. Also let us know if your parents or some other person will be with you. We have a special program to acquaint guests of prospective students with our staff and facilities during the on-campus visit.

                              Sincerely yours,
                              ↓4

                              Arlisle Marneffe
                              Admissions Office
                              ↓2

srs
Enclosure

The tasks in Unit 8 (Lessons 44–49) will review typing activities of Units 5, 6, and 7. You may want to refer back to these units as you complete these tasks.

PART TWO

In Part Two you will learn how to display letters, cards, and tables. You will also learn how to compose at the typewriter using rough-draft correction symbols. The final unit in Part Two will integrate all the job problems you typed in Units 5, 6, and 7.

Part Two has four units. Unit 5 (Lessons 26–31) will introduce you to note-cards, reference cards, and postcards. Unit 6 (Lessons 32–37) will further develop your ability to use the proofreader's marks that were shown in earlier lessons. You will be able to type a wide variety of letters, both personal and business—the kinds of letters you will be typing in the future and perhaps even now while you are in school. Unit 7 (Lessons 38–43) shows you how to center tables vertically and horizontally. Your skill at composing will be used in developing and typing tables in this unit. Large and small envelopes will be illustrated so you will now be able to type a letter and an envelope for all your correspondence. Unit 8 (Lessons 44–50) is a little different—it is an "integrated" unit. A theme runs through several lessons. Your first theme or project will be writing and composing letters and postcards to obtain information from a college you plan to attend after high school graduation. The second project will involve a typing survey. You will write a letter, postcards, and a table before completing this project.

When you have completed Part Two, you will be able to:

1. Use proofreader's marks.
2. Type an informal personal letter, a formal personal letter, a personal business letter, and a letter using a letterhead.
3. Type reference and notecards, postcards, and envelopes.
4. Display tables using correct vertical and horizontal placement for the table and the column headings.
5. Compose a variety of letters and tables.
6. Type 30 words a minute for 3 minutes with 4 or less errors.

goals

Type 29 wam for 3 minutes. ☐ Type a business letter and envelope. ☐ Learn letter placement according to number of words in body.

> **TYPING TIPS**
> ☐ Spell out numbers from 1 through 10; use figures for numbers above 10.
> ☐ Use all figures—even for numbers 1 through 10—in expressions of money (*$6*), percentages (*8%*), and dimensions (*4 by 5 meters*).

◗ **50-space line; single-space; each line three times or more; double-space between** *different* **lines.**

WARMUP

1 Take extra care as you drive on very snowy roads.
2 The white wine poured slowly from the old bottle.
3 Each pair of shoes cost $24.99 plus 4% sales tax.

Insert vowels.

4 If y—— will load —t in th— tr—ck, —'ll dr—ve too.
$|_1$ $|_2$ $|_3$ $|_4$ $|_5$ $|_6$ $|_7$ $|_8$ $|_9$ $|_{10}$

LONGHAND SPRINT

◗ **Type from longhand. If you finish one line in 12 seconds, your speed is 50 wam.**

5 *My dog was the best of all those up for adoption.*
6 *Christmas shopping is hard on the feet and purse.*
7 *Decorations need to be put in the gym by four.*

SKILL CHECK

◗ **Try to type 29 words a minute for 3 minutes with 4 or fewer errors.**

8   Shuffleboard is a game played on some smooth   10
9 surface such as pavements, wood flooring, or ship   20
10 decks. An official court spans 52 feet long by 6   30
11 feet wide. The object of the game is to propel a   40
12 wood or metal disk into a scoring area and bounce   50
13 the disk of the rival out of the way. Players use   60
14 a long stick with a curved head to steer the disk   70
15 to score.   72
16   Senior citizens as well as others on board a   82
17 ship quickly excel at it.   87
$|_1$ $|_2$ $|_3$ $|_4$ $|_5$ $|_6$ $|_7$ $|_8$ $|_9$ $|_{10}$ **SI: 1.26**

goals

Type 23 wam for 3 minutes within 4 errors.
☐ Type on 4″ x 6″ cards.

┌───┐
│ TYPING TIP   │
│ ☐ Use commas to set off the year in complete dates, e.g., │
│   March 1978, but March 17, 1978.   │
└───┘

◐ 50-space line; single-space; tab 5; each line three times or more; double-space between *different* lines.

WARMUP

1 Was Jim's prize for boxing quickly given by Thad?
2 Zoe has 18 days to make 34 hats for 25 new clubs.
3 The girls and the boys had not seen them box yet.

Insert vowels.

4 Wh—n c—n yo— f—ll th— b—xes f—r th— sen——r cl—ss?
  |1 |2 |3 |4 |5 |6 |7 |8 |9 |10

◐ 30-SECOND SPEED CHECK

5 You may have watched many boxing matches thinking   **10**
6 that it is an American sport. It really began in   **20**
7 Ancient Greece and Rome, and it was very popular.   **30**
  |1 |2 |3 |4 |5 |6 |7 |8 |9 |10

PRACTICE UP REACHES

◐ Use directions for Warmup.

8 by on am but cob six but lack cone five able vine
9 be an me lab vie mix job mind jump game camp live
10 in my ax bag vex dab cam many save hand fame vane

SCORING

An easy way to figure your speed for a timed writing is to read the last superior number that you passed. For example, if you finished line 16, your speed is 20 wam. To score 23 wam, you must finish line 17.

SKILL CHECK

◐ Try to type for 3 minutes at 23 words a minute.

11   Much of the equipment of a boxer has changed   **10**
12 since the sport began. Early Greeks fought bare—   **20**
13 handed; later they used leather thongs with metal   **30**
14 studs for an added thrill. Romans wore a smooth,   **40**
15 hard glove on each hand. Bare-handed fights were   **50**
16 back in style for a time, but a prizefighter just   **60**
17 has to wear gloves now to protect the hands.   **69**
   |1 |2 |3 |4 |5 |6 |7 |8 |9 |10   **SI: 131**

ADDRESSING ENVELOPES

▶ **Refer to the illustrations on the bottom of page 83 as you read Steps 1 to 4 below.**

1. *Return address.* If not printed, it begins on line 3, single-spaced, blocked 5 spaces from the left edge. If the return address is printed, type the name of the writer above the printing, aligning it with the top line of printing. The personal title *Mr.* is omitted, but other personal or professional titles can be used.

2. *On-arrival directions. Please Forward, Confidential, Personal,* and *Attention Mary Smith* are typed on line 9 in capital and small letters, underscored, 5 spaces from the left edge, to align with the return address.

3. *Addressee's name and address.* On a small envelope (No. 6¾ or its metric equivalent, C7/6), begin on line 12, 2 inches from the left edge. On a large envelope (No. 10 or its metric equivalent, DL), begin on line 14, 4 inches from the edge. Always use single spacing and blocked arrangement. City, state, and ZIP Code must be on the same line. State name may be spelled out or abbreviated; the post office prefers the two-letter abbreviations.

In a foreign address, indicate postal zone (if known) after city, and type the name of the country in all capitals on a separate line.

4. *Special mail service.* Type the appropriate notation (such as SPECIAL DELIVERY or FIRST CLASS) in all caps in the upper right corner of the envelope, beginning on line 9. The notation should end about 5 spaces from the right margin.

▶ **43-1. Using slips of paper cut to the sizes indicated in the illustration on page 83, type a large envelope and a small envelope for the letter in Task 41-1 on page 81 and the letter in Task 42-2 on page 82. Send Task 41-1 *Special Delivery.***

▶ **43-2. Type a large envelope and a small envelope for each of the handwritten addresses given below.**

① Mrs. Jean Ingabrand
40 Tolver Drive
Franklin, OH 45005

② John W. Santiago, Editor
World News Tribune
Jacksonville, FL 32206
(Mark Personal)

③ Registrar
California College of Arts
2948 Broadway
Oakland, CA 94618
(Send Special Delivery)

④ Dr. Felix J. Mortimer
University of Southern Indiana
14 Peachtree Drive
Troy, IN 47588
(Mark Please Forward)

⑤ Dr. Nicholas P. Georgiady
Clinica Cubana
60-79 Fourth Avenue
Miami, FL 33170

⑥ Mrs. Sally Wong
The University of British Columbia
20 Westbrook Drive
Vancouver, B.C. V6T 1W5
CANADA
(Send Registered)

▶ **Type the tasks below on 4″ x 6″ cards. For Task 26-1, double-space after author's name and after publication data, including pages. Use the miniatures at left for placement suggestions.**

26-1. (Reference card) Church, Olive. SHADOW MOUNTAIN LODGE, Typing Practice Set. McGraw-Hill Book Company, New York, 1978, 240 pages. A do-it-yourself typing practice set placed in a large hotel-resort operation. Includes instruction booklet, business forms, envelopes, carbon paper, folders, and index cards. Typing jobs relate incidents involving hotel guests and employees and a mystery that is eventually solved.

26-2. (Notecard) POINTS TO REMEMBER WHEN OPERATING A LAWNMOWER. 1. Filter the gasoline before putting it in the mower. 2. Check the oil before starting the mower. 3. Disengage the blades when removing the clipping bag. 4. Turn off the choke when finished mowing. 5. Clean clippings from blades before putting mower away.

26-3. (Reference card) Use this typing textbook as a reference and compose another card similar to the one you typed in Task 26-1.
26-4. (Notecard) Compose a list of the things that you need to remember in order to operate your typewriter skillfully. Refer to Task 26-2.

27

goals

Type 23 words a minute for 3 minutes within 4 errors. □ Type on 3″ x 5″ cards.

TYPING TIPS
□ Ordinarily, leave 2 spaces after the period that follows a number or letter in a list.
□ If a list consists entirely of one-line, single-spaced items, leave only 1 space after the period.

▶ **50-space line; single-space; each line three times or more; double-space between *different* lines.**

WARMUP

1 Max amazed Jeth by quickly answering five points.

2 Jayne (the girl next door) is an excellent sport.

3 Kevin can smash the ball with speed on the court.

Insert vowels.

4 H—w m—ny po—nts d—d th—y sc—re f—r th— l—st g—me?
|1 |2 |3 |4 |5 |6 |7 |8 |9 |10

▶ 30-SECOND SPEED CHECK

5 The Irish brought handball to America, and it has   10

6 been a very popular indoor exercise for about one   20

7 hundred years. Do you know how to play handball?   30
|1 |2 |3 |4 |5 |6 |7 |8 |9 |10

8   Canoeing can provide an exciting way to move   10

9   in the back country and a good way to gaze at the   20

10   lake streams. It takes both skill and safety for   30

11   a canoe trip to be a pleasure. Since a canoe can   40

12   upset very quickly when it is not balanced, it is   50

13   important to make adjustments to avoid this. The   60

14   equipment used will depend upon the type of trips   70

15   you are taking. Sometimes canoes are rigged with   80

16   sails or with motors.   84

|1 |2 |3 |4 |5 |6 |7 |8 |9 |10   **SI: 1.34**

FOLDING LETTERS

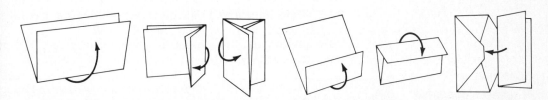

Folding a letter for a small envelope. Bring bottom up to ½ inch from the top . . . fold righthand third toward left . . . fold lefthand third toward right . . . insert last crease into the envelope first.

Folding a letter for a large envelope. Fold up the bottom third of the paper . . . fold the top third over the bottom third . . . insert last crease into the envelope first.

Charles B. Larson
1783 Mariners Lane
Stamford, CT 06902

REGISTERED

<u>Personal</u>

     Ms. Eileen M. Haden
     234 Neponset Street, Apt. 3B
     Worcester, MA 01606

Jose Malinas
Box 740, Rural Route #2
Rockford, IL 61102

SPECIAL DELIVERY

     Hayes & Stiles, Inc.
     56 Dickinson Street
     Springfield, IL 62704

No. 6¾ is 6½ by 3⅝ inches. The metric equivalent, measuring 220 by 110 mm, is referred to as *C7/6.*

No. 10 is 9½ by 4⅛ inches. The metric equivalent, measuring 162 x 81 mm, is referred to as *DL.*

8 nip saw can mop got day way sip zoo hut wool feel

9 few hop jaw old bet hip sew lap bat sad kiln fast

10 red tax imp gas dip ion mat let rob top wait calm

11 farm home game time drop grew jump view trip ripe

12 same read crop head aqua limp true sail free help

13 veil lion text quip tote trim blip vote film mild

SKILL CHECK

▶ Your goal is still 23
words with 4 or less
errors—can you do it?

14   Handball is an activity that gives the whole   10
15 body a way to gain exercise. Each player is very 20
16 intent on jumping back and forth zinging the ball 30
17 against the walls with quick motions. A court is 40
18 one, two, three, or four walls, but four walls is 50
19 the most popular type. A rubber ball is used for 60
20 bouncing against the walls in rhythmic style.   69

|1 |2 |3 |4 |5 |6 |7 |8 |9 |10   **SI: 1.30**

▶ **Type the tasks below on 3″ x 5″ cards. Use the miniatures at the left for placement suggestions.**

KRISPY MARSHMALLOW TREATS
(Use microwave oven.)

1/4 cup butter or margarine
5 cups miniature or 40 large
marshmallows
5 cups crispy rice cereal

Setting: HIGH

1. Melt butter 1 minute in glass baking dish.
2. Stir in marshmallows; bake for 1 minute;
   stir until smooth.
3. Mix in cereal.
4. Cool until set.

Calando, Robin

392 Abbey Way
Dayton, OH 45459

Phone: 433-8945

27-1. (Recipe card) KRISPY MARSHMALLOW TREATS. (Use microwave oven.) $\frac{1}{4}$ cup butter *or* margarine, 5 cups miniature *or* 40 large marshmallows, 5 cups crispy rice cereal. Setting: HIGH. 1. Melt butter 1 minute in glass baking dish. 2. Stir in marshmallows; bake for 1 minute; stir until smooth. 3. Mix in cereal. 4. Cool until set.

27-2. (Address cards) Robin Calando, 392 Abbey Way, Dayton, OH 45459, Phone 433-8945. Sheri Wells, 58039 Patriot Square, Dayton, OH 45419, Phone 433-9930. Laiying Chang, 36 Whipp Road, Dayton, OH 45429, Phone 433-6894.

27-3. (Recipe card) Choose a recipe of your own and type it on a card to give to a friend. Use Task 27-1 as an example.

27-4. (Address cards) Type your own name, address, and telephone number and that of two friends on three different cards. Use Task 27-2 as an example.

8   Judo is an art which requires the use of the   10
9 body and mind in a skillful way. Although it has   20
10 its origin in Japan, judo is now known throughout   30
11 the world. Judo involves a complex system with a   40
12 goal of training the mind and body for fitness in   50
13 many ways. Students of judo are trained to think   60
14 and analyze the moves before they make them. All   70
15 kinds of degrees can be earned in the practice of   80
16 truly skillful judo.   84

|1 |2 |3 |4 |5 |6 |7 |8 |9 |10   **SI: 1.34**

COMPOSING A LETTER AND TABLE

You are a sophomore in college and your younger brother or sister writes to you about what he or she should be packing for college next year.

▶ **42-1. Make up a table of at least 15 items that would be needed. Arrange them in three columns.**

▶ **42-2. Compose a letter to accompany the suggested list. The letter should be average in length, containing at least three paragraphs.**

goals

Type 28 wam within 4 errors. ☐ Learn how to fold letters. ☐ Address 2 sizes of envelopes.

TYPING TIP
☐ On the last line of an address for an envelope, leave only one space between the state and the ZIP code, e.g., Detroit, MI 48221.

▶ **50-space line; single-space; each line three times; double-space between *different* lines.**

|1 |2 |3 |4 |5 |6 |7 |8 |9 |10

WARMUP

1 Will you fix the zoom lens in her camera by five?
2 The bank will pay 6½% for $500 or 7½% for $1,000.
3 He knows that you can take a canoe trip anywhere.
4 *It was quite a joke how she dodged the big party.*

PREVIEW THE SKILL CHECK

5 can way very lake trip both with this since skill
6 gaze provide upset balanced adjustments outboards
7 safety rigged quickly canoeing pleasure equipment

28

goals

Type 23 wam for 3 minutes within 4 errors.
☐ Type 4″ x 6″ and 3″ x 5″ cards.

TYPING TIP
☐ Use the apostrophe for feet and quotation marks for inches in technical references:

Type the index on 3″ x 5″ cards.
The room is 25′10″ x 16′6″.

▶ 50-space line; single-space; each line three times or more; double-space between *different* lines.

WARMUP

1 Bad fog may jinx Zeke's trip to watch live quail.

2 Jerry has won 24 trophies in 1978 and 36 in 1979.

3 Skill in using a rifle takes a lot of practicing.

Insert vowels.

4 H—nting —s — v—ry —njoy—bl— sp—rt f—r som— f—lks.
|1 |2 |3 |4 |5 |6 |7 |8 |9 |10

▶ 30-SECOND SPEED CHECK

5 Hunting can be done with a camera as well as with   10

6 a gun. Many people enjoy the choice prizes found   20

7 on film more than ones captured by bow or bullet.   30
|1 |2 |3 |4 |5 |6 |7 |8 |9 |10

PRACTICE RIGHT-HAND WORDS

▶ Use directions for Warmup.

8 pin you lop nun ohm ink oil ply ill pup noun Polk

9 joy him hip mop non hip hum pop lip hum July milk

10 lop Jim mom Hun pun Jon Lon Mil nil Min upon Jill

11 look only hill lump lion hook oily punk poll pull

12 loon luny hunk honk jump lily limp John kink junk

13 holy poly hull lump monk puny pill mill yolk pump

SKILL CHECK

▶ You should be able to type 23 words a minute with 4 or less errors easily now.

14   Hunting began as an event that was important   10

15 for survival. Today much of the hunting which we   20

16 do is just for sport. There are as many kinds of   30

17 hunting as there are parts of the world. Some of   40

18 the most exciting hunting involves big game and a   50

19 lot of exotic equipment. But whether it is zebra   60

20 or quail, the thrill of a hunter is the same.   69
|1 |2 |3 |4 |5 |6 |7 |8 |9 |10   SI: 1.33

41-1. Business Letter: 5-inch line; indent paragraphs. Type a line of hyphens across the sheet on line 7 to simulate a letterhead.

(Today's date) Ms. Lara Sindona, 348 Warrington Drive, Morehead, KY 40351

Dear Ms. Sindona:

Thank you for your inquiry about the collection of children's literature available in our library. We are now able to provide an entire section for books for young children.

During this past month, Mr. Poole, our assistant librarian, has composed a list of children's books which he would like to add to our collection. We hope to add several of them this year.

To give you some idea of which books you might want to donate, I have enclosed Mr. Poole's list of suggested books. We shall appreciate any books that you may want to donate, however, whether they are on this list or not. Sincerely, Shelley Russo, Librarian URS Enclosure

41-2. Table. Center on full page; double-space.

CHILDREN'S LITERATURE COLLECTION

Books to Be Added

Author	Title
Comfort, Iris	Let's Grow Things
Emerson, Caroline	All in a Day's Work
Koehler, Cynthia	This Magic World
Landis, Dorothy	My Flower Book
Lear, Edward	The Nonsense Alphabet
Pierce, June	My Poetry Book
Spyri, Johanna	Heidi
Wadsworth, Wallace	Choo-Choo
Wilkin, Esther	So Big

42

goals

Type 28 wam within 4 errors. ☐ Compose an original letter and table.

TYPING TIP
☐ If a table is to appear on a page by itself, it should be centered horizontally within the established margins and also centered vertically on the page.

50-space line; single-space; each line three times; double-space between _different_ lines.

WARMUP

1 Just watch Fred's van zip by those exits quickly.
2 Our new yearbook, Elk Tales, won national honors.
3 This is an art which uses both the mind and body.
4 *You will learn to make those graceful moves, too.*

PREVIEW

5 mind with goal many ways them move them judo body
6 requires origin Japan throughout involves degrees
7 complex system analyze training skillful practice

▶ Type these two tasks on 4″ x 6″ cards. Use the miniatures at the left for placement suggestions.

28-1. (Notecard) USING NOTECARDS FOR SPEECHES One of the most common uses for notecards is to make notes for reference when giving a speech. Key words may be listed in outline form, to identify main topics and subtopics. Key words may also be listed simply in numerical order. How much detail is typed on the card depends upon the speaker's needs. These words cue the speaker to ideas that he or she wants to present and develop in the talk. The larger cards (4″ x 6″) are usually used so that speakers can handle them with ease.

28-2. (Reference card) Sabin, William A., THE GREGG REFERENCE MANUAL, Fifth Edition, McGraw-Hill Book Company, New York, 1977, 326 pages. This manual is a complete guide for writers, typists, and transcribers. It presents the basic rules that apply in business writing, and offers many examples and illustrations to serve as models.

29

goals

Type 24 wam for 3 minutes within 4 errors.
☐ Type messages on reference, index, and postcards.

> TYPING TIP
> ☐ When a quotation occurs within a sentence as a *non-essential* expression, use a comma before the opening quotation mark and before the closing quotation mark:
>
> The next chapter, ''The Role of Government,'' further clarifies the answer.

▶ 50-space line; single-space; each line three times or more; double-space between *different* lines.

WARMUP

1 A quick jab will never cause Zoy to flex or push.
2 Mary's new article, "Checkmate," was not printed.
3 I know that Lee will call soon about the new inn.

Insert vowels.

4 If h- ch-se - pet, w---ld -t b- a d-g -r - rabb-t?

|1 |2 |3 |4 |5 |6 |7 |8 |9 |10

goals

Type 28 wam for 3 minutes within 4 errors.
□ Use appropriate displays for transmitting data.

TYPING TIPS
□ To review styling elements for tables:
□ Title of Table—all caps, centered
□ Subtitle of Table—caps and small letters, centered
□ Column Heads—caps and small letters; center over the column text. Underscore each line of the column head.

▶ **50-space line; single-space; each line three times; double-space between _different_ lines.**

WARMUP

1 Did you ever watch anyone when they were gliding?
2 "I can," said Sally. "I can, too," yelled Freda.
3 It is such a quick and graceful kind of movement.
4 *Banji can analyze their mix by pouring it slowly.*

12-SECOND SPRINTS

▶ **Type each line twice.**

5 You can learn how to make it go up and then down.
6 It is a fine day for us to go for a balloon ride.
7 The ride can be very smooth if the pilot is good.

8 The wind may decide which way the girls can ride.
9 Our boys want to take a trip over the green lake.
10 It is exciting to zip through the air by balloon.

SKILL CHECK

▶ **Try typing 28 words a minute for 3 minutes.**

11   Imagine gliding smoothly above the earth and   10
12 sea in a lazy fashion. As the air in the balloon   20
13 expands, it goes higher in the sky. A valve pump   30
14 controls the weight of gas inside the balloon and   40
15 it quickly moves through the air. Since the wind   50
16 goes in different directions at different levels,   60
17 some mark of control can be made by adjusting the   70
18 balloon to that height where the wind may blow in   80
19 a way you want to go.   84

SI: 1.32

5 Did you know that chess is now a sport in league 10
6 play for many high schools? Students compete to 20
7 earn points for the schools all during the year. 30

|1 |2 |3 |4 |5 |6 |7 |8 |9 |10

▶ **Use directions for Warmup.**

8   mill pass hoop cuff pool miss need door deer tell
9   jeep free boss well jeer lass ball dill peep moss
10 seem rook weep eggs boss tees mall less will feed
11 skill happy small skeet broom sleep battle differ
12 spill merry foggy happy small furry oppose bottle
13 occur funny dizzy offer adder issue puzzle sizzle

SKILL CHECK

▶ Try to type 24 wam
for 3 minutes within 4
errors.

14   Chess is a game of skill played with a king, 10
15 a queen, two bishops, two knights, two rooks, and 20
16 eight pawns. The ultimate goal of any chess game 30
17 is to force the surrender of an opposing player's 40
18 king. This is called a "checkmate" and it brings 50
19 the game to an end. Chess demands the ability to 60
20 analyze moves before they are finally made on the 70
21 chessboard. 72

|1 |2 |3 |4 |5 |6 |7 |8 |9 |10   **SI: 1.34**

▶ **Follow the instructions outlined below.**

```
Ernest Toro
489 Stephanie Lane
Centerville, OH 45459


       Mr. Gary Weidner
       Director of Admissions
       The Ohio State University
       78 Circle Drive
       Columbus, OH 43210
```

ADDRESSING A POSTCARD

1. Single-space and block all lines.
2. Start the return address on line 3, $\frac{1}{2}$ inch from the left edge. It is common practice not to use a title in a return address. However, if the writer prefers a title for identification (such as Ms., Mrs., Dr., or Rev.), it is proper to include it.
3. Type any special directions (like "Please forward") on line 9, $\frac{1}{2}$ inch from the left edge.
4. Start addressee's name and address on line 12, 2 inches from the left edge.

```
                December 20, 19--

Dear Mr. Weidner:

I visited your College of Arts and Sciences
this past week and was very impressed with the
opportunities available.  As a high school
senior, I am now trying to decide which college
to attend.  Would you please send me your bro-
chure about the College of Arts and Sciences
and an application form for admission to the
university.  Thank you very much for your
assistance.

                Ernest Toro
```

TYPING THE MESSAGE

1. Use single spacing.
2. Start date at center of line 3.
3. Have side margins of about $\frac{1}{2}$ inch.
4. Type closing lines on second line below last line of message. Align closing with date.
5. To leave a bottom margin of 3 lines, omit if necessary: complimentary closing, handwritten signature, and reference initials.

5 smash watch drive guess right when drop game what
6 badminton worldwide shuttlecock volleying playing
7 quickly exactly serving indoors points recognized

8   What a smash! Watch out for that drop. Did   10
9 you see that drive? Guess what they are playing?   20
10 If you said badminton, you are exactly right. It   30
11 is a game played quickly indoors and out. All it   40
12 takes is two rackets, a shuttlecock, and a net to   50
13 begin the volleying from side to side. Only when   60
14 a side is serving can it score points. This game   70
15 is recognized worldwide because it's an enjoyable   80
16 sport.   81

|1 |2 |3 |4 |5 |6 |7 |8 |9 |10   **SI: 1.30**

COMPOSING TABLES

▶ Compose these ta-
bles, remembering the
four steps for compos-
ing:

Outline
Draft
Edit
Retype

40-1. Assume that you are in charge of setting up the room assignments for a speech tournament in your school. Using the following names and room numbers, design and type an appropriate table. Mary Isaac, Dawn Taulbee, Robert McCluskey, Lea Dunitz, Al Esposito, Myra Babinski, and Ted Schramm are the speakers. Rooms available are 120C, 122C, 124C, 117D, 234D, 236D, and 136E. Your table needs a title and column heads, too.

40-2. You are part of the stage crew for a musical, and you have borrowed a number of props. Compose a table listing the props and their owners. Chair, Marvin's Furniture; rug, Sarah Knee; planter, Town Flower Shoppe; lamp, Ella Morawski; curtains, Mrs. DeMarco; radio, Paul Rytone; bicycle, Larry Storen; bookcase, Jim Boggs; and pictures, Julia Renaldo.

40-3. Imagine that you are going to take a field trip with your biology class. There are 15 students going in 4 cars to Grant Life Science Center on November 8, 19—. Compose a table displaying this information. Use names of your friends and classmates; be sure that you have a title, subtitle, and column heads.

29-1. Type a message and address on a post-card following the directions on page 60.

(From) Ernest Toro, 489 Stephanie Lane, Centerville, OH 45459 (To) Gary Weidner, Director of Admissions, The Ohio State University, 78 Circle Drive, Columbus, OH 43210 (Message)

(Today's date) Dear Mr. Weidner: I visited your College of Arts and Sciences during this past week and was very impressed with the opportunities available. As a high school senior, I am now trying to decide which college to attend. Would you please send me your brochure about the College of Arts and Sciences and an application form for admission to the university. Thank you very much for your assistance. (Typed name) Ernest Toro

30

goals

Type 24 wam within 4 errors. ☐ Type addresses and messages on postcards.

> TYPING TIP
> ☐ Use the two-letter state abbreviation in addresses. Leave one space between the state abbreviation and the Zip Code:
> Abbeville, SC 29620
> Mokapu, HI 96734

▶ 50-space line; single-space; each line three times or more; double-space between *different* lines.

WARMUP

1. Jack has the exact size club to fit my short arm.
2. Type these pairs in reverse: 01, 92, 83, 74, 65.
3. Bo can play golf with Quin at the new club today.

Insert vowels.

4. Jan c-n h-t th- b-ll w-th--t - chip if sh- tri-s.

12-SECOND SPRINTS

▶ Have someone time you once for exactly 12 seconds on each of these sentences.

5. I think that you will be able to do it very well.
6. I know that you can do it if you work hard at it.
7. Some skills take more time than they should take.

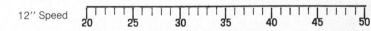
12″ Speed

Every stroke counts as a word on the scale. For example, if you typed to *a* in *able* in line 5, you typed 26 words a minute.

8. When can you play golf with me at the new course?
9. You can hit balls from the driving range at noon.
10. They can play one round of golf after we go home.

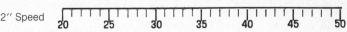
12″ Speed

ing that is narrower than its column, determine the difference between the heading and the longest entry in the column. Divide that number in half (drop any fraction) and indent the column heading that many characters. (Example: Event = 5; Javelin Throw = 13; $13 - 5 = 8 \div 2 = 4$. Indent 4.)

3. *To center column headings wider than columns.* When a column head is wider than its column, first determine a key line using the column head. (Example: Varsity Cheerleaders = 20; Squads = 6; 20 + 6 + 6 empty spaces = 32.) Backspace from the center and type the headings. To set the left margin for column 1, subtract the longest entry from the heading, divide by 2, and indent that many spaces. (Example: Varsity Cheerleaders = 20; Jill Frankenfeld = 16; $20 - 16 = 4 \div 2 = 2$. Indent 2 spaces from heading and set left margin.

▷ 39-1. Table With Column Headings Shorter Than Columns.

TRACK RECORDS

For Men

Event	Distance
High Jump	7' 7 1/4"
Pole Vault	18' 8 1/4"
Long Jump	29' 2 1/2"
Shot Put	72' 2 1/2"
Discus Throw	232' 6"
Javelin Throw	310' 4"

▷ 39-2. Table With Column Headings Longer Than Columns.

FALL SPORTS

Varsity Cheerleaders	Squads
Bill Zinck	1
Aida Perlo	1
Jill Frankenfeld	1
Fran Hahn	2
Joe Fazio	2
Susan Feeback	2
Marilyn Kapecky	3
Enzo Caliandro	3
Anita Jung	3

goals

Type 27 wam within 4 errors. □ Compose some tables of your own.

TYPING TIP
□ If the table requires rules, any of these methods may be used:

Insert all rules on the typewriter, using the underscore.
Insert all rules with a ball-point pen and a ruler after the typing is done.
Insert all horizontal rules on the typewriter; insert vertical rules with a pen.

▷ 50-space line; single-space; each line at least three times; double-space between *different* lines.

|1 |2 |3 |4 |5 |6 |7 |8 |9 |10

WARMUP

1 Allen can serve it over just as quickly as Alexis.

2 Peg scored 2, Zoe has 6, Lee has 4, and Jay has 2.

3 He will smash the bird if he is closer to the net.

4 *It is a sport which you can play with two or four.*

```
11        Grab your golf clubs and head for the greens    10
12   in fine style.  You will be joining lots of other    20
13   men and women who are engaged in a sport that can    30
14   offer great exercise and fun at the same time.  A    40
15   challenge of traps, trees, bushes, sand, and wind    50
16   quickly intrigues the wits of all.  You will soon    60
17   realize the kind of joy felt from a zestful round    70
18   of golfing.                                          72
```

|1 |2 |3 |4 |5 |6 |7 |8 |9 |10   **SI: 1.22**

TYPING MESSAGES
AND ADDRESSES ON
POSTCARDS

▶ Cut 3 strips of paper, 5½″ wide by 3¼″ long, to simulate postcards for Tasks 30-1—30-3.

30-1. (From) Your name and address (To) Miss Theresa A. Monk, 1090 Spring Court, Apartment K, Preston, MO 65732 (Message) (Today's date) Dear Theresa: I am finally settled in my new job and find that it is quite challenging. My new apartment is just two blocks from the hospital and not very far from a small shopping center. (New paragraph) Please drop me a line when you have a chance. My new address is: 95 Allen Boulevard, Apartment S, Urbana, MO 65767 (Your name)

30-2. (From) Your name and address (To) General Manager, Holiday Hotel, Las Vegas Boulevard, Las Vegas, NV 89101 (Message) (Today's date) Dear Sir or Madam: I made a reservation for July 28 thinking that this would be the date that my friends and I would be on our way to California. We now find that the correct date is July 29. Please change my reservation to July 29 with all the room accommodations remaining the same. May I please have a confirmation of this date as soon as possible. (Your name)

30-3. (From) Your name and address (To) Dr. Carlo Marinelli, Department of Business Education, University of Michigan, Ann Arbor, MI 48107 (Message) (Today's date) Dear Dr. Marinelli: Our business club is planning a program for March 18, 19—, which will include a discussion of "New Trends in Business Education." You have been highly recommended as a speaker on this topic. Would you please let me know whether you could meet with our club on March 18. (Your name) Secretary, Wayne High Business Club

goals

Type 27 wam for 3 minutes within 4 errors. □ Learn how to type tables with subtitles and headings.

50-space line; single-space; each line three times; double-space between *different* lines.

WARMUP

1 You will be amazed when you fix a place for them.

2 We saw 8 robins, 2 doves, 5 wrens, and 1 bunting.

3 A bird will give much joy to those who take time.

4 *Seeds and berries offer good food for wintertime.*

PREVIEW

5 may own birds maybe learn plant kinds group daily

6 want take acquire studying notebook watch special

7 boxes sizes enjoy learn camera attract protection

SKILL CHECK

See if you can type 27 wam with 4 or less errors.

8   If you enjoy studying birds, you may want to   10

9 take a walk with a camera and a notebook. If you   20

10 like to watch birds from your own home, maybe you   30

11 will want to learn how to attract birds. One way   40

12 is to plant special kinds of trees and shrubs for   50

13 food and protection. Another way is to acquire a   60

14 group of feeders and nesting boxes where they can   70

15 live. Birds of all sizes look for these shelters   80

16 daily.   81

SI: 1.26

COLUMN HEADINGS

Column headings are usually centered, but they may be blocked. If they are blocked, of course there is no centering problem. If they are centered, procedures vary according to whether the column headings are shorter or longer than their columns.

1. *To block column headings.* Block column headings only for informal use and only if all headings for a table are shorter than their columns. Simply start the column heading where the column entries begin.

2. *To center column headings narrower than columns.* To center a column head-

31

goals

Type 24 wam for 3 minutes within 4 errors.
☐ Identify and use revision marks to revise copy.

▷ **50-space line; single-space; tab 5; each line three times or more; double-space between *different* lines.**

WARMUP

1 What is the jumbo text I must study for the quiz?

2 The book cost $13.40, and it came from S & L Inc.

3 Does it take very much skill to learn to whistle?

Insert vowels.

4 Ye—rs —go, a m—n w——ld fenc— t— def—nd h—s h—n—r.
|1 |2 |3 |4 |5 |6 |7 |8 |9 |10

▷ **12-SECOND SPRINTS**

5 Let him go to the game if he can go with the men.

6 It is best to do what you can when you can do it.

7 It is easy to know if you have learned the skill.

12″ Speed 20 25 30 35 40 45 50

8 Would you like to see them when they are fencing?

9 Which part of the body can be the most important?

10 It can be hard work to make one goal in the game.

12″ Speed 20 25 30 35 40 45 50

11 It is the women who learn to fence with the foil.

12 Does she think that a saber would be hard to use?

13 Have you seen the epee used for a fencing weapon?

12″ Speed 20 25 30 35 40 45 50

SKILL CHECK

▷ **Try 24 wam for 3 minutes with 4 or less errors once more.**

14 If you would like to experience a unique bit 10

15 of sport which has been known for centuries, give 20

16 fencing a try. It is a skill that is prized, and 30

17 it is enjoyed by both men and women. The goal of 40

18 the game is to touch the opponent on a particular 50

19 part of the body without being touched in return. 60

20 Three weapons are used: the foil, the saber, and 70

21 the epee. 72

|1 |2 |3 |4 |5 |6 |7 |8 |9 |10   **SI: 1.31**

PARTS OF A TABLE

Title. Center the title and type it in all capitals.

Subtitle. Leave 1 blank line below the title and center the subtitle. Capitalize principal words. Leave 2 blank lines after a main title if there is no subtitle (as in 38-1 and 38-2).

Column Heads. Leave 2 blank spaces between the subtitle and column heads. Center each column head over its column. Capitalize principal words.

Body. Leave 1 blank space below column head for body (column entries). Normally leave 6 spaces between columns and center body horizontally on the page.

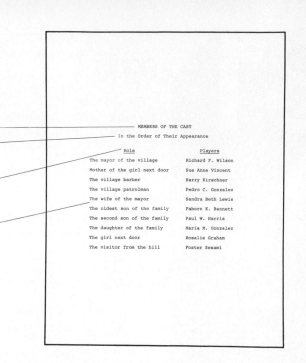

STEPS IN TYPING MULTI-COLUMN TABLES

1. *Clear the machine.* Move margin stops to the extreme left and right of the carriage; clear tab stops.

2. *Compute top margin.* Find on what line to type the title to center the table vertically (see page 34). Insert the paper to that line and center the carriage or carrier.

3. *Select the "key line."* Find the longest entry in each column; add 6 spaces between columns; this is the key line. (Example: Sonny Jurgenson + 6 + Fran Tarkenton.)

4. *Set left margin.* From the center, backspace as if to center the key line and set the left margin.

5. *Set column 2 tab stop.* Tap the space bar once for each character in the longest entry for column 1 and for the 6 spaces between columns 1 and 2. Set a tab stop at that point.

6. *Set additional column tab stops.* Space over to next column (tap the 6 blank spaces) and set a tab stop at the start of the next column. Do any additional columns in the same manner.

7. *Type the table.* Backspace-center the title (remember to lock the shift key), drop down 3 lines, and type the body of the table.

▶ **38-1. 2-column table; center on a full page.**

FAMOUS FOOTBALL PLAYERS

George Blanda	Steve O'Neal
Jim Brown	O. J. Simpson
Roman Gabriel	Bart Starr
Paul Hornung	Fran Tarkenton
Sonny Jurgenson	John Unitas
Joe Namath	Bob Waterfield

▶ **38-2. 3-column table; center on a full page.**

CLASSICAL COMPOSERS

Bach	Dvorak	Schubert
Beethoven	Haydn	Stravinsky
Berlioz	Liszt	Tchaikovsky
Brahms	Mahler	Vivaldi
Debussy	Mozart	Wagner

Use this chart of revision marks, commonly used by typists, writers, proofreaders, and editors, as a reference for completing Tasks 31-1 and 31-2.

Mark	Description	Example		Mark	Description	Example
∧	Insert word	and it	ss[	Use single spacing ..	and so it	⌣	Join to word	the port
⌐	Omit word	and so it	∿	Turn around	ss had it so	word	Change word	and if he
....	No, don't omit	and so it	ds[	Use double spacing.	ds and so it white=hot	○	Make into period......	to him()
\	Omit stroke	and sob it	=	Insert a hyphen		○	Don't abbreviate	Dr Judd
/	Make letter small	And so it	⌐	Indent — spaces......	s If he is	○	Spell it out.............	① or ② if
≡	Make a capital........	if he is	⋕	Insert a space..........	andso it	¶	New paragraph	¶ If he is
≣	Make all capitals.....	I hope so	⌇	Insert a space..........	andso it	✓	Raise above line	Halel says
⌐	Move as indicated....	and so⌐	⌒	Omit the space	10 a m.	+⋕	More space here......	It may be
≡	Line up, even up......	TO: John	__	Underscore this	It may be	-⋕	Less space here.......	If she is
‖	Line up, even up......	‖ If he is	⌒	Move as shown	it is not	2⋕	2 line ...	It may be

31-1. Revise "Hints for Correcting Errors by Erasing," making corrections according to the revision marks indicated. Use a 50-space line. Type the list on a half-sheet of paper.

Hints for Correcting Errors by erasing

1. # Turn the paper so that the error will be at the top of the cylinder.

2. Move the carriage far to the left or right (use margin release) to make eraser grit fall outside the typewriter.

3. Press the paper tightly against the cylinder with the left fingertips.

4. With a typewriter (INK) eraser, erase each letter to be deleted. Use quick, light strokes and blow eraser grit away. *or brush*

5. Turn back to the writing line and type corrections

6. ‖ Insert correction.

31-2. Type the paragraph on a half sheet of paper. Double-space, and make the corrections that are indicated. If you make any errors, follow the steps for correcting errors by erasing.

5 If you would like to experience a unique bit of sport which has been known for centuries, give fencing a try. It is a skill that is prized, and it is enjoyed by both men and women. men. The goal of the game is to touch the opponent on a The goal of the game is to touch the opponent on a particular part of of the body with out being touched in return. # ③ weapons are used: the foil, the sabre, and the epee.

officer of professional business organizations. Would your schedule permit you to address our Business Teacher Education Club on the subject of professionalism for the business teacher? We have a limited budget, but we could pay you an honorarium of $100. (Paragraph) Our meeting will begin at 7 p.m. on November 11 in Carter Hall on our campus. We look forward to your acceptance of our invitation. Sincerely yours, Mary Jane Grabar, President. MJG:rw

goals

Type 27 wam for 3 minutes within 4 errors. □ Learn how to display communications in table form.

TYPING TIPS
□ Before typing any tabular material, plan the horizontal and vertical placement carefully.
□ If the table is to appear on the same page with straight copy, it should be centered horizontally and should be set off by one to three blank lines from the text above or below.

▶ **50-space line; single-space; each line three times; double-space between *different* lines.**

```
      |1    |2    |3    |4    |5    |6    |7    |8    |9    |10
```

WARMUP

1 Did she quit racing and jumping her lively horse?

2 They will meet us at 4:30 near 2961 First Avenue.

3 He can fix my bike so that it will zip up trails.

4 *Riding is a skill which requires many long hours.*

▶ **30-SECOND SPEED CHECK**

5 We can ride our bikes on some of the trails which   10

6 lead to the open land near the pond. That curved   20

7 trail would be a fun place to try a short sprint.   30

```
      |1    |2    |3    |4    |5    |6    |7    |8    |9    |10
```

SKILL CHECK

▶ **27 words a minute with 4 or less errors is your goal.**

8   Whether you are six or sixty, you will enjoy   10

9 the fun that goes with a bicycle ride. Feel that   20

10 breeze in your hair and the power in your feet as   30

11 you glide down one grade and push rhythmically up   40

12 the next one. If you can ride where there are no   50

13 cars whizzing by, you can experience the peaceful   60

14 feeling invited by the quiet country trails and a   70

15 trickling stream lurking here and there. Who can   80

16 wait?   81

```
      |1    |2    |3    |4    |5    |6    |7    |8    |9    |10   SI: 1.25
```

goals

To compose at the typewriter. □ To increase skill in typing from longhand notes. □ To type 25 wam for 3 minutes within 4 errors.

TYPING TIP
□ Ordinarily, a man should not include *Mr.* in his signature. However, if he has a name that could also be a woman's name (Leslie, Adrian, Lynn) or if he uses initials (F. L. Palo), he should use *Mr.* in either his handwritten or typewritten signature.

▶ **50-space line; single-space; tab 5; each line three times or more; double-space between *different* lines.**

WARMUP

1 I found some lazy bones in my quest for exercise.
2 If you work hard and dream less, you will profit.
3 Column 2 should show each #4 crate selling @ $12.

Insert vowels.

4 Th— hot s—n q—ickly dr——d my h—ir —ft—r sw—mming.

|1 |2 |3 |4 |5 |6 |7 |8 |9 |10

TYPING FROM LONGHAND

▶ **Try a 2-minute writing on longhand copy.**

5 Get a good, sturdy pair of running shoes and
6 zip around the block five or six times just after
7 you get up. If you pace yourself carefully as to
8 speed and distance, you will find that jogging is
9 quite satisfying to give you pep for the new day.

▶ **Use directions for Warmup.**

AIM FOR ACCURACY

With practice on right-hand drills

10 ion action notion ration potion onion lions scion
11 you youths you're bayous you've young bayou yours
12 ply supply simply comply damply imply reply apply
13 joi joints adjoin joiner joined joins joint joist

BUILD SPEED

With practice on alternate-hand drills. After you have typed these drills, see the top of p. 20 to check the quality of your typing.

14 air stairs flairs chairs fairer pairs lairs fairs
15 rid riddle bridge riders bridal rides bride pride
16 pan pantry pander panics sampan panda panel pangs
17 han handle change hanger shanty handy thank shank

37

goals

To type a business letter using a letterhead. □ To type 26 wam for 3 minutes within 4 errors.

▶ **50-space line; single-space; each line three times or more; double-space between *different* lines.**

WARMUP

1 A stream of red juice oozed from the huge bottle.

2 Raindrops quietly fell on the tin roofs overhead.

3 Later on in 1976, one pound was worth only $1.55.

Insert missing letters.

4 Tickets f—— the all-school pl—y s—ld o—t by n——n.

|1 |2 |3 |4 |5 |6 |7 |8 |9 |10

SKILL CHECK

▶ **Try to type 26 wam or more in 3 minutes with 4 or fewer errors.**

After typing this 3-minute timing, you may want to go back to page 65 and practice either the speed or accuracy lines.

5 Frank: I just finished a term paper on the topic   10

6 of volleyball for my phys ed class. You may be a   20

7 bit surprised at some things I learned when I did   30

8 the theme. For example, did you realize that the   40

9 game has existed since 1900? Were you aware that   50

10 a person from this country invented the game? It   60

11 is now quite well liked as a sport and is popular   70

12 in as many as 60 countries of the world.   78

|1 |2 |3 |4 |5 |6 |7 |8 |9 |10   **SI: 1.32**

BUSINESS LETTER

▶ **On a plain sheet of paper, type a "letterhead," setting up the lines as shown. Begin on line 7, at 20 on the carriage or carrier scale for elite and at 12 for pica, and double-space. Then type the letter—5-inch line; single spacing; tab at center; date on line 13.**

B U S I N E S S   T E A C H E R   E D U C A T I O N   C L U B

Indiana State University

South Bend, IN 46608

October 10, 19—. Dr. James Eastman, Professor, Business Education, Leeds University, Pittsburgh, PA 15217. Dear Dr. Eastman: Our advisor, Dr. Helen White, has recommended you as an experienced member and

Letterhead

Initials of writer and/or typist—2 spaces below writer's name and title

USING THE TYPEWRITER FOR CREATIVE WRITING

The first step in creative writing is to *outline* in pen or pencil a guide to what you will write. The outline may be very detailed, or it may be just a list of key words that are arranged in sequence. The preparation of this outline involves thinking, planning, and perhaps researching for the data you want to include in what you write.

The second step in creative writing is to *draft* the composition. Use the typewriter for this step. Type your ideas as rapidly as you can, referring to the guide for your clues. Type rapidly; do not stop for corrections; get your ideas on paper! To provide ample room for subsequent editing, use double-spacing and a short line of writing (a 50-space line is just about right).

The third step is to *edit* your draft. Read the draft to see if your ideas are presented clearly; if not, revise them to improve the presentation. Then read for errors in typing and spelling, and review the arrangement. Mark corrections as you read and review. Using pen or pencil, polish your quickly written first draft.

The fourth step is to *retype* your work in correct form, being sure to make all the corrections marked on the draft. Now is the time to type carefully, to avoid making errors. Then proofread carefully and correct any errors that might have slipped in.

32-1. COMPOSING AT THE TYPEWRITER

▶ Full sheet; double-space; 50-space line. Read the question, think briefly about your answer, then type and compose it at the same time. Write simple, complete sentences. Edit and rewrite as you go along.

1. What is the point of preparing an outline for a report or a theme?

2. What should you include in an outline?

3. Do you find that you make many or few revisions on drafts of papers you write?

4. Do you like to write papers? Explain why you do or do not.

SKILL CHECK

▶ Try to type at least 25 wam for 3 minutes within 4 errors.

```
18      Mountain climbing is a very difficult but an    10
19  interesting sport.  It requires special equipment   20
20  and skills.  Those who take part in this exercise    30
21  must be in superb health and prepared for a major    40
22  task.                                                41
23      On some sharp climbs, climbers rope each one     51
24  together for protection as they wind up through a    61
25  maze of rock, ice, cold, and snow until a peak is    71
26  finally in full view.                                75
```

|1 |2 |3 |4 |5 |6 |7 |8 |9 |10   SI: 1.34

① 5-inch line; single-space; tabs at 4 and center; begin on line 13.

This letter is shown in pica type.

Inside address—the name and address of person receiving the letter.

"Hanging" numbers stand at the margin; a run-over line is indented 4 spaces.

"Enclosure" is typed at the bottom of a letter if something accompanies it in the same envelope.

A postscript expresses an afterthought. Begin it at the left margin. Type PS: before the first word.

R.R. 3, Box 10
Bloomington, IN 47401
October 4, 19--
↓5

Mr. J. M. Reed, Manager
Sunset Trailer Court
3800 Main Street
Delay Beach, FL 33444

Dear Mr. Reed:

Mrs. Brown and I are planning a trip to Florida the latter part of January in our travel trailer. We should like a reservation for a two-week period at your court, beginning Monday, January 23. We desire the following arrangements:

1. A lot location that will permit a drive-through parking area for a 25-foot trailer.

2. A lot location that will be far enough away from the game rooms to permit a quiet surrounding.

3. Electric and water hookups for the trailer.

Enclosed is my check for $25 to serve as a deposit.

Sincerely yours,
↓4

John Russell Brown
↓2

Enclosure
↓2
PS: Please return the check if you cannot take care of us.

33

goals

To increase speed on short timings. ☐ To increase skill of composing at the typewriter. ☐ To type 25 wam for 3 minutes within 4 errors.

▶ **50-space line; single-space; tab 5; each line three times or more; double-space between *different* lines.**

WARMUP

1 Juice containers range from small to extra large.

2 When things are cheap, we have no money to spend.

3 Give me 20 $10 bills in exchange for 40 $5 bills.

Insert vowels.

4 Wh—n w—ll th—y t—ll y——r a—nt th—t y——r te—m w—n?
|1 |2 |3 |4 |5 |6 |7 |8 |9 |10

BUILD SPEED

With practice on: words with double letters

5 ee sleepy steely fleets eerie steep needs heel ee

6 pp happen topple supper happy dippy pappy supp pp

7 ss misses vessel classy dress bossy press mass ss

8 ll willow sullen filler allow still shall will ll

9 All vessels in the fleet will need mess supplies.
|1 |2 |3 |4 |5 |6 |7 |8 |9 |10

down reaches

10 in in inner pinch again plain ruin rain pain into

11 ex ex expel extol exile exist exit next apex flex

12 om om omits omega women homes omen dome comb whom

13 The exit and domed apex of the tomb are in ruins.
|1 |2 |3 |4 |5 |6 |7 |8 |9 |10

CARD INVITATION

You are in charge of the activities committee for your Total School Involvement Association. You must send a card announcing a special program to every member of the faculty inviting them to attend without charge a dinner program honoring your retiring principal. You have been fortunate to secure as your speaker the governor of your state who will pay recognition to the principal, a longtime friend of the governor's. This very special event will be April 23 at 6 p.m. at the King's Inn. You must prepare a card to send to faculty.

36

goals

To type personal business letters. ☐ To type 26 wam for 3 minutes within 4 errors.

▶ **50-space line; single-space; each line three times or more; double-space between** *different* **lines.**

WARMUP

1 Quizzical Joe the bee buzzed around the wax buds.

2 To build speed in typing, push your fingers hard.

3 At the beginning of 1976, one pound was worth $2.

Insert missing vowels.

4 O-r flo-t won f-rst pr-ze in th- ann-al carn-v-l.

|1 |2 |3 |4 |5 |6 |7 |8 |9 |10

LONGHAND SPEED SPRINTS

▶ **Type as rapidly as you can from longhand.**

5 *The boss has yet to obtain an invoice on the vat.*

6 *The ugly, inky spot ought to dry fast in the sun.*

7 *A sturdy willow tree was planted in the new mall.*

8 *Use an oar if it appears the wind is not blowing.*

SKILL CHECK

▶ **Try to type 26 wam for 3 minutes within 4 errors.**

9   Rugby football is a fast, rough sport played   10

10 by two teams. American football is very close to   20

11 it. The goal of both is the same: to run, pass,   30

12 or kick an oval ball over a maze of bodies joined   40

13 as a solid wall to tackle the ball carrier. Each   50

14 half has a fixed 40-minute time for play.   58

15   Each game is rough, but rugby players wear a   68

16 fair amount of equipment to protect their bodies.   78

|1 |2 |3 |4 |5 |6 |7 |8 |9 |10

SI: 1.28

▷ 33-1. Follow the steps outlined below.

Step 1. Jot down notes on what you need to include on the card. The notes may be brief and in handwriting, something like this:

Special event. Governor will attend. To honor retiring principal. All faculty invited.

Step 2. Prepare a first draft. Set your margins for a 4½-inch line. To allow room for editing in Step 3, use double spacing. You need to compose only the body, for you can insert the date, salutation, and closing lines later, when you type the final product. You have space on the card for 8 lines at most. Example:

            I am thrilled to
announce that . . . .
        All faculty of our
school . . . . We plan to
honor our retiring . . . .
This special event will be
held on . . . at . . . .The
location is . . . .

Step 3. Edit the draft. Go over your work carefully, marking every improve ment it needs: Spelling? Capitalizing? Punctuating? Indenting? Correct time, date, and place? Limited to 8 lines of typing?

Step 4. Now type the complete card. Adjust to single spacing and remember to type the date, salutation (Dear Mr. —— or Dear Ms. ——), and closing (be sure to use your title).

▷ 33-2. If time allows, draft your card again, in the form of a display announcement. Refer back to page 36 to review the form.

Refer back to page 36

SKILL CHECK

▷ Try to type 25 wam for 3 minutes with 4 or fewer errors.

14   Polo is a ball game played by persons riding   10
15 horses.   The rules of the game are very much like   20
16 hockey.   There are four persons on each team with   30
17 an objective of driving the ball through the zone   40
18 of the rival team to score.   46
19   The players take a cane or mallet to hit the   56
20 ball while riding a horse.   The joint strength of   66
21 rider and horse must mix to acquire a victory.   75

SI: 1.24

▶ 5-inch line; single-space; tab at center; begin on line 13.

Read this letter *before* you begin to type. It has facts you need to know about typing a personal letter.

This letter was done in elite type.

The miniature below shows how the letter would appear on 8½" x 11" paper.

(Most people do not type their name below the signature space in an informal letter.)

SKILL CHECK

▶ Try to type 26 wam or more in 3 minutes with 4 or fewer errors.

Writer's address ——————————————
124 Southview Avenue
Narrows, VA 24124
Dateline ——————————————
October 9, 19--

Omit address of
person to whom
you are writing

Salutation ———————— Dear Helen:

This letter illustrates a standard arrangement for an informal
personal letter to a friend.

The top margin should be at least 2 inches deep, and so the
return address is begun at the center of line 13. Having a
tab stop there will help. Leave four blank lines before the
salutation.

Body ————————
It is acceptable to indent each paragraph five or ten spaces,
but most typists prefer the style shown here.

Informal personal letters are single-spaced unless you know
that the body will be very short; in this case you can stretch
the letter by double-spacing the body. If you double-space,
you must indent paragraphs.

Start the closing at the center, two lines beneath the body.
If you wish to type your name under the signature space, drop
down four or five lines and align it with the closing, like
this:

Closing ————————————————————————— Cordially,

Writer's name —————————————————————————— John R. Elliott

```
11  John:  Lacrosse is the name of a sport taken from       10
12  the Indians of Canada.  The game is played in the       20
13  eastern part of our country as well as in Canada.       30
14  Lacrosse is to some extent like field hockey.  It       40
15  requires ten players for a team.  They use a long       50
16  stick that has a net at the end.  The net is used       60
17  to seize the ball, and very quickly a player must       70
18  get it past the opponent's goalposts.                   78
```

SI: 1.25

goals

Continue to develop composing skill. ☐ Type 25 wam for 3 minutes within 4 errors.

▷ **50-space line; single-space; tab 5; each line three times or more; double-space between *different* lines.**

WARMUP

1 A giant blaze was quickly quenched by the expert.

2 Try not to make the same error as you go to work.

3 The tagged numbers (40 & 60) were the sale items.

Insert vowels.

4 Dick h–d t– p–y d–ty f–r th– fur h– g–t f–r June.
|1 |2 |3 |4 |5 |6 |7 |8 |9 |10

COMPOSING EXERCISE

▷ **Review the four steps for composing on page 66; then try your skill at developing one or both of the following ideas into a story. Step 1 is completed for you. Follow through in developing Steps 2, 3, and 4. Type your final story in paragraph form.**

34-1. Outline for Step 1.

Saw an old man drop a $20 bill.
Picked it up and thought "Finders keepers."
Felt very guilty.
Ran after man, returned the money.
He was very grateful because . . . .
(Provide your own ending.)

34-2. Outline for Step 1.

Went camping in woods with two friends.
Pitched tent.
Heard rustling sound.
Thought it was a bear.
It turned out to be . . . .
(Provide your own ending.)

BUILD SPEED

With practice on in motions

5 ad adds admit arm ark army arrow able about above

6 ace act acre aver avow avail pie pin print pianos

7 put puff purse Pyrex pyramid photo phrase physics

SKILL CHECK

▶ Try to type 25 wam or more in 3 minutes with 4 or fewer errors.

8   One of the popular games enjoyed in the home   10
9 is Ping-Pong, which is known too as table tennis. 20
10 The game is indeed like lawn tennis but on a very 30
11 small scale. A 9' x 5' table is used. The table 40
12 is divided by a net into two equal parts. 48
13   It takes two people for singles, or four for 58
14 doubles. Each player has a small, wooden paddle. 68
15 A light ball, small size, is used. 75

|1 |2 |3 |4 |5 |6 |7 |8 |9 |10   **SI: 1.30**

goals

To type an informal personal letter. □ To type 26 wam for 3 minutes within 4 errors.

TYPING TIP
□ When writing the name of a person in an inside address or elsewhere in a letter, be sure to follow that person's preferences in the spelling, capitalization, and spacing of the name.

▶ 50-space line; single-space; each line three times or more; double-space between *different* lines.

WARMUP

1 An empty box, next to the 4-quart bucket, is new.
2 All Things Wise and Wonderful is a story of love.
3 I have read pages 2, 9, 35, 38, 46, and 50 today.
Insert vowels.
4 Th- -ld m-n g-t o-t th- b-g n-w b-x f-r th- l-dy.

|1 |2 |3 |4 |5 |6 |7 |8 |9 |10

BUILD SPEED

With practice on up and down reaches

5 sky joy set lab jet are pet coy sue lot join lard
6 went lint like junk myth live hymn even sent went
7 jump hurt quit axle raze gone time vine poke able
8 fast dart safe rate were rest vest cast wart axes
9 tart cave west vast save best card bare feed fate
10 web fad gas wet get few war sat bed red gage bear